D1649927

History's Greatest Spies

The Hidden Story of Richard Sorge

Conrad Bauer

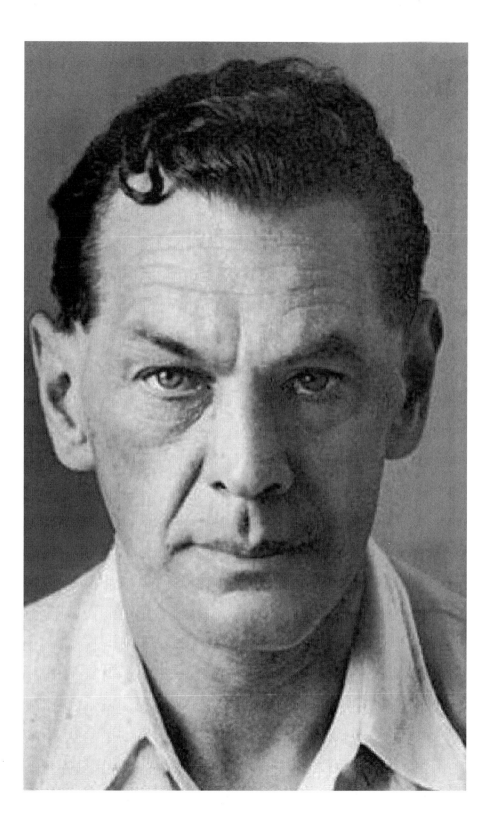

ISBN: 978-1981299126

Printed in the United States

MAPLEWOOD
– PUBLISHING –

Contents

Introduction

It can be easy to think of spies just as we see them in the movies. All of the high-speed car chases, the witty one-liners, and the femme fatales feed into a common conception of an international man of mystery. But real spy work is different. Real spy work is, ultimately, human. It is conducted by flawed men, exploiting the fear and ambition of similarly damaged individuals. At the end, the credits do not roll. Spies are far likelier to find themselves caught and executed in a foreign land than they are to drive off into the sunset with a new paramour on their arm. Real spies are real people, and they are in real danger at all times.

Even if the popular conception of a spy might be fundamentally flawed, it does not mean that the actual equivalents are not just as exciting. The intelligence gathered can have world-changing significance and can save – or threaten – millions of lives. Of all the spies that ever lived, the greatest is a man named Richard Sorge. As the Soviet Union's best intelligence officer, he went deep undercover as a Nazi in Imperial Japan. The information he gathered had a real impact on the course of human history. The true story of his life is, in the classic sense, stranger than fiction.

In this book, we will explore key events from the life of history's greatest spy. We will learn how he gathered intelligence, turned informants to his will, and fooled everyone with whom he fell into contact. But we will also learn of his flaws, his tragedies, and his final demise. If you would like to learn what it takes to become a real spy, read on and discover just how high the bar has been set.

The Early Life of a Spy

Sorge during World War I in 1915

Like all of the best stories, this one starts at the beginning. The early life of a spy starts much in the same way as many other children. If we want to know about the man who Richard Sorge became, we have to understand how his circumstances conspired to perfectly place him as a future weapon of one of the world's greatest superpowers.

A Far-Flung Corner

As part of what is now Azerbaijan, not many people know where Baku actually is. In 1895, it was a small slice of the Russian Empire as ruled by Nicholas II. At the time, Russia and its huge empire were caught between the feudalism of the old world and the growing reality of the new European order. The Napoleonic Wars and the following decades of turmoil had hinted at the changing pace of politics and warfare on the continent, with Russia seemingly relegated to a sideshow as the other European countries moved ahead. Russia's considerable size was both her greatest power and greatest weakness. The sheer scale of the country produced a wealth of natural resources and a large population, but modernization and movement into the industrial age were delayed. Other than the cities closest to the West, the majority of the country was struggling to keep up with the times. This was true in Baku and many corners of the Empire. Though Nicholas II would attempt to renovate and reinvigorate many corners of the nation, he would never be able to complete his mission.

The settlement of Sabunchi was fairly remote, even by Russian standards. A major source of oil, however, it was an important part of Russia's attempts at modernization. If the country was to power its way into the Twentieth Century, it would need fuel. The Caucasian Oil Company (named for the nearby Caucus Mountains) was the major player in the area and employed many of the local population. Among them was a German immigrant who had moved to the area. Wilhelm Richard Sorge was a mining engineer who had been tempted to move to an isolated part of the Russian Empire. He had a lucrative contract that payed him well and a Russian wife, Nina Semionovna Kobielevawho, who provided him with nine children. The youngest of these took Wilhelm's middle name, Richard.

But the family's time in the region would not last. After Wilhelm's contract with the Caucasian Oil Company expired, he and his wife decided to move back to Germany. Young Richard was only a few years old at the time, but – as he would later admit – the knowledge that he was born in Russia before moving to Germany would have an important influence on his later life. Together, the family moved to Berlin. Though large families were common during this period, nine might still have been considered a high number of children. Even when in Baku, the family had tended to speak German on a day-to-day basis.

Looking back into the family tree, Richard's grandfather – Friedrich Adolf Sorge – was a known associate of Freidrich Engels and Karl Marx, who would found the Socialist Workers Party in the USA. This fact – like much of Richard's childhood – would later be seized upon by his Soviet biographers. There was a slight mistruth, however, in that Friedrich Sorge was actually Richard's great uncle (rather than grandfather) and had never actually been that close to the Communist writers. This slight modifying of the truth would be a returning motif in the life of the man who would become his country's greatest spy.

But that was still in the distant future. In Germany, with Richard just eleven years old, the family was well off, living comfortably in a residential part of Berlin. Remembering his own version of school, Sorge recalls that he could be a difficult student but had more than enough interest in a few subjects to show real promise. Literature, history, and social sciences were the topics that truly caught his eye and in which he excelled, so much so that the other children in his class took to calling Richard "the Prime Minister." By fifteen, he was utterly engrossed in history, in particular the aftermath of the Napoleonic Wars and the work of Otto von Bismarck. This fed into an understanding of contemporary events, and the young man – half Russian, half German – began to educate himself on current affairs.

Roger's father, Wilhelm Sorge, died in 1911. However, his death did not result in the family becoming poor. Their vacation in Sweden in 1914 is demonstrative of the fact that the family was able to live comfortably without their patriarch. As with most life in Europe in 1914, however, everything was set to change. The outbreak of the World War I meant that Richard Sorge was thrust into the army at a young age, swept up in a heady mix of excitement, patriotism, and an urge to see what geopolitics were like up close. Having described his teenage existence as "the whole meaningless and purposeless pattern" typical of 18-year-olds, the war was a chance to see something new. It was unclear at that point just how different this war would become.

A Taste of War

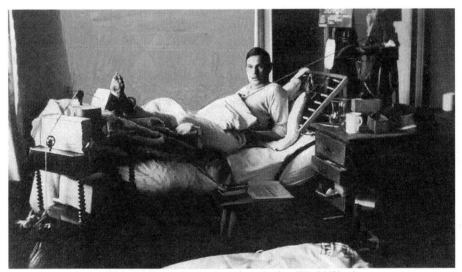

Richard Sorge in the hospital, during World War I

Sorge's first six weeks as a soldier were spent suffering through the inadequate training regime of the German army. Despite possessing one of the greatest armed forces of all time, there was a sudden realization that the nation would require a large volume of troops to supplement the well-oiled war machine that was currently marching through Belgium, the group Sorge was soon sent to join. In no short time, the excitement and wonder of the war wore off. It was in the army when he first encountered a pacifist. Describing the man as a "real leftist," Sorge remembered the impact that the man's stories about persecution and unemployment left upon an impressionable teenager. The man, a stonemason from Hamburg, died in 1915.

A short time later, while serving in the bloody battle at Ypres, Sorge was wounded. Sent back to Germany to heal, he discovered a different world to the one he had left behind. In wartime Germany, the black market facilitated the purchase of almost anything. Money was the key. Any excitement the country had held at the outbreak of war had vanished, gone the same way as the young boy's own hopes. Sorge began to note the imperialist, economic, and material motivations of his government and its rivals. Any kind of war in Europe, the government said, would be eradicated through the establishment of German domination.

Sorge made attempts to study at university but found himself disenfranchised with life in Berlin. He found himself preferring life back in the trenches with the men who he described as "naïve brothers in arms." Healed, he volunteered for frontline duty once again and returned to the war in time to see the German army destroy the Russian forces. Sorge moved with them, returning for the first time to the country where he had been born. This time, he was an invading force. The Germans' advancement into Russia seemed never ending, with countless miles racked up as the Russian army retreated ahead of them. It added to the sense of eternal conflict, the idea that the war itself was endless. For Richard Sorge, however, a second injury would curtail his time in the land of his birth. Returning to Germany once more, he began to pass through the occupied Russian territory.

Richard Sorge would return to the frontlines a third time, but it would be his last. In Baranovichi, to the south of Minsk, he found himself on the receiving end of a barrage of shrapnel as a shell fell nearby. The fragments tore into his body, smashed bones in his leg and left him with a limp for the rest of his life. He would always feel a dull, nagging pain from the aftereffects of the blast. As luck would have it, the doctors and nurses who treated him at Konigsberg were ardent socialists, and noting the potential within Sorge, began to provide him with political writing. They encouraged him to return to the studies he had originally abandoned.

A New Revolution

Sorge was in a huge amount of pain following his injury but turned once again to the subjects that had fascinated him as a boy; the fine arts, economics, philosophy, and history. He consumed all of it at a voracious rate. For the first time in years, he thought of himself as happy. Once he was healed, he left the hospital well-read and filled with a newfound spirit of revolution. Buoyed by this new love of academia, he returned to university. His earlier medical studies were thrown out in favor of political science. A growing disillusionment with the war was furthered by the loss of two of his brothers and millions of deaths on either side. Germany was an economic mess, he believed, and was falling apart at the seams. However, neither the losing German side nor their victorious opponents were in better shape. The war had ruined everyone.

From this darkness and during his studies, Sorge found himself an ideology he described as "fresh and effective." Not only did this new set of beliefs preach revolution, but they also wanted to end this war and future wars. While he was studying at university, he found himself digging deeper and deeper into the beliefs. A short time later, news of the Bolshevik revolution in Russia broke.

The stories about a communist revolution in the country of his birth hit Sorge hard. There was a sudden urge not only to support the revolution in theory, but also to take up arms and become a real part of the movement. Discharged at last from the army in 1918, he went first to the university in Kiel and joined up with the Independent Social Democratic Party, where he helped recruit members, agitated against the government, and lectured on Marxism. Chief among his students were dock workers, sailors, and others who found themselves at the harbor.

His studies were not over, however, and in 1919 Richard Sorge moved to Hamburg to complete his Ph.D. in political sciences. After finishing the course in less than a year, he returned to party activity and became a member of the German Communist Party, which had since risen up and subsumed other, similar groups. In his new position, he worked as a training chief in Hamburg and helped to advise the local communist newspaper. Later, he took on a new job as a miner at the party's behest in order to spread the word among the miners. He was eventually discovered, having made the political climate in the area far more intense, and encouraged to leave. A suggested move to Holland fell apart after his reputation preceded him.

Attempting to unravel Richard Sorge's own account of his growing obsession with communism is tough. As well as the minor mistruths he was happy to spread, his work often required that he cover up his own activities and hide away the truth about what he had been doing. Throughout the 1920s, he had been studying under a man named Dr. Kurt Gerland, who became something of an ideological mentor to the young Sorge. By 1921, however, Sorge had fallen into a romantic relationship with Gerland's wife, and after what was described as an "amicable divorce," Sorge married the woman. This was the first of a series of women whom Sorge would encourage to fall in love with him. Though he may not have known it at the time, the seduction of his mentor's wife would pave the way for a slew of romantic entanglements that would become a key factor in his career as a spy.

Shortly after 1922, when Sorge was still deeply engrained in the party, Germany outlawed the Communist Party. This forced many of the members underground. This can be seen as one of the first introductions into the world of secret espionage that Robert would encounter. As the liaison between Frankfurt and the Berlin headquarters of the party, he was responsible for secret messages, propaganda, and the control of the party's funds and register of members. We have reports from this time that Sorge's home was at the very center of this social circle. There was apparently a mixture of "serious talk" with the more relaxed "lust for living."

This life would change when Sorge accepted a position as a bodyguard for the visiting members of the Comintern. The organization was based in Moscow and encouraged the mobilization of communist activities around the world, with the hope of prompting further revolution. As a bodyguard for high-ranking members, Sorge was also expected to take part in (sometimes violent) revolutionary activity. Such was his performance in the role that he was invited to join an intelligence bureau based out of the Comintern headquarters.

And so, with the German Communist Party's approval, the couple travelled to Moscow in late 1924. By the beginning of 1925, Sorge had thrust himself into the new role. He became an official member of the Soviet Communist Party and a citizen of the country. This change was kept hidden from the officials back in Germany. He retained his German passport and continued to use it while travelling.

For the next four years, attempting to determine Richard Sorge's activities remains difficult. While we know he began to learn the ropes of international espionage, he did so in a manner that left very little in the way of provable activity. What we do know, we have gathered together from scraps, rumors, and legends. During this time, for all intents and purposes, Sorge simply vanished from the public view that he had previously enjoyed.

Undercover

We can gather that the first two years of Sorge's career as a Soviet citizen were spent in Moscow, working out of the headquarters of the Comintern. He played a key role in the expansion of the group's intelligence division and used his time in the Russian capital to indulge himself in the ideological material provided to him by the party. Rather than the romantic idea of a revolutionary reading illicit material away from the government's gaze, he was now ensconced in the world's largest communist nation, and the material he had previously taken such pleasure in reading was now entirely state-sanctioned. As well as refining his political learning, he worked hard on his language skills and polished up his abilities in both English and Russian. Despite being born in Russia, he and his family had spoken German in the household. It was now time to relearn the language.

Another clue as to how Sorge spent his time can be learned from the writings he produced during this period. He authored two books, both on the subject of the history of economics. The first focused on the Treaty of Versailles and how its provisions affected the "international labor class." The second was a rumination on the history of German imperialism. When reviewing the works, Sorge thought them to be "competent."

Sorge's wife, Christine, struggled with the move to Moscow more than her husband. Having found work at the nearby Marx-Lenin Institute, it quickly became clear to her that she did not care for the local people. Christine was able to note – as many might have done in 1925 – that the rising star of one Joseph Stalin was bringing with it an increased sense of intolerance and an oppressive atmosphere. Locals considered her to be bourgeois and shunned her. She began to resent her husband's fondness for alcohol, for women other than herself, and for his continued neglect of her wellbeing. Christine asked her husband for permission to return to Germany. Sorge obligingly waved goodbye from the platform of the station.

Christine's reflections on the state of the marriage and on her husband's indiscretions are a key insight into her husband's mental condition, and though she rarely gave exact details, it can be seen to lay the ground work for much of the behavior that Sorge would exhibit as a spy. She did note that, when Sorge encountered a woman who he could not bend to his will – for reasons of morality, legality, or simply social – he chose to levy an insult against them, referring to these women as "bourgeois geese."

But that is not to say that she did not love her husband and that she did not remain fond of him even after her departure. Though she would eventually immigrate to America, she did not marry in later life and always maintained correspondence with her former husband via letters. There is little to suggest that the two ever went through the legal procedure of a divorce, but we do know that Sorge considered himself to be a single man and decided that married life, such as he had experienced it, was not for him.

Perhaps this was down to the fact that he was able to get sexual gratification from outside the confines of his marriage. To women, it seemed, he constantly managed to exude a mesmerizing, seductive, and alluring quality. Frequently, his comrades would suggest to him in piques of envious bemusement that he might consider the possibility of settling down. But Sorge would simply grin, batting away the suggestion with a glib remark about how he was not built for the happiness of a traditional marriage.

Now without even a wife to worry about, Sorge was freer than ever to delve deeper and deeper into the world of espionage. He had already familiarized himself with the craft and had begun to gain a realization that true intelligence (in an espionage sense) was about the supplementation of the data he had acquired with real, genuine firsthand information for agents on the ground. The Comintern network had long been able to help local communist parties in other countries organize and solve structural problems. They were now considering the idea of using these smaller parties to form the basis of an intelligence network, dispatching agents to teach these locals how to correctly set about the world of intelligence gathering.

Sorge was one of the primary agents in this field. The bosses at the Comintern sent him all over Europe to both engage in intelligence-gathering opportunities regarding the communist parties and to evaluate economic and political problems in the respective nations. In addition, he was to note any military issues that he might encounter, ones that might be of interest to the USSR.

When we examine the evidence Sorge has provided for his own whereabouts during this time, it does not tally with information from other sources. Whether he was travelling in Norway, Sweden, or Denmark, later investigations – such as that by the Germans – would conclude that he had rarely been present in the countries when he claimed to have been so. There are two ways in which we can thus treat Sorge's claims. First, we might surmise that Richard Sorge invented his time travelling across Scandinavia in order to provide cover for an entirely separate mission (perhaps one that took place in Germany.) Alternatively, we might be able to conclude that those who conducted the investigations – for example, the German police – simply confused Richard Sorge with a man of the same name, or where not able to track him correctly. Even if there is little evidence for his actual whereabouts during these years, we can say for certain that he was, at one point, in Germany. Once there, he recruited Hede Massing, who would later write about the experiences the two shared.

Espionage as a whole became more and more of a fascination for Robert Sorge. Increasingly, the need to cater to the political requirements of his job began to grate more and more. A trip to Great Britain in 1929 saw this frustration reach a fever pitch and Sorge informed his superiors that he felt the political and intelligence aspects of his work could not actually be considered homogenous. In order to accomplish his espionage goals, he must work in complete secrecy. This was not possible while fulfilling his political envoy requirements. The high command at the Comintern began to see things from his perspective. In response, they severed all ties with Richard Sorge. They required that he, in turn, sever all ties outside of professional requirements with any other members of the organisation. There were a few exceptions, men such as Manuilsky, Kuusinen, and Pyatnitsky, who all remained in contact with Sorge in their capacity as unofficial advisors.

As well as breaking contact with the Comintern, Sorge sought to break away from any political party cells with whom he had been in contact. He delved further and further into the world of Soviet espionage, becoming a member of the organisation known as the Secret Department of the Soviet Communist Party Central Executive Committee. He was required to make contact with one of the spying community's leading figures, General Ian Antonovitch Berzin, who was chief of the Fourth Department of the Red Army. The Fourth Department was the Red Army's intelligence division and had essentially been founded by Berzin, who had heard through his professional contacts of Sorge's desire to become a full time intelligence officer and to take part in political espionage on behalf of the Soviet Union.

Sorge's reputation and prior work was of such a high standard that he was given a choice of assignments. Having been accepted into the Fourth Department, he was asked whether he would prefer to return to

Europe or to travel instead to the Far East. Sorge, with his constant curiosity already alerted by the potential offered on a new continent, chose the latter. This was perfectly in line with his superiors' wishes, as they now had an agent of the highest quality to dispatch to one of the most problematic regions in the world. The huge amount of political turnover and upheaval in the region meant that the potential for communist activity was high. If the Soviet Union were to help light the touch paper on the explosion of worldwide communist revolution, then this might be the perfect place to start. Sorge chose to move to China, considered at the time to be the 'heart of Asia.' Once there, he was given the task of establishing, organising, and operating a Red Army network of spies in the city of Shanghai. After years of wandering almost aimlessly, Richard Sorge finally had a real purpose in life, one that he knew he loved. He was now, officially, a spy.

A Soviet Spy

Sorge in 1940

Richard Sorge did not move straight to Shanghai. Now a Soviet Spy, his cover needed to be slightly more complex. Thanks to the secrecy of the last few years, Sorge had learned to speak English. With his experience in a number of newspapers, he took on a cover story as an American journalist sent to report on events in China, where his accent might not be questioned. Transforming himself, Sorge was taking the first steps towards his future position as history's greatest spy.

Across the Sea

Shanghai of the late 1920s was a diverse city. As well as the original Chinese area and the French section, there was an international zone of sorts, housing people from across the world. As one of the Pacific's major ports, it was not unexpected to see people from all over the globe walking through the streets. Preparing to depart for Shanghai, Sorge travelled first to Marseilles before boarding a cruise ship set for Japan. It would be January, 1930, before the ship made port in Shanghai.

But Sorge was not alone aboard the vessel. With him were two other operatives, men who would become key figures in the emergent intelligence network. The first was named Seppel Weingarten, an expert in radio communications. The second was simply known by the code name 'Alex' and was considered to be the superior officer to Sorge in both age and time spent in service to the party. Together, they were required to report on any information they might find of the Chinese government's actions in Nanking. This included the military strength in the area, the political and social characteristics of the city, and the foreign and domestic politics as they came to light. In addition, information on Chinese industry and agriculture was to be gathered. There existed opposition factions in the region, people unenthused with the British and American activities in China. Information about these groups was also to be acquired, while data regarding the military capacity of foreign countries stationed in the area was of interest to the Soviets. Finally, there existed a need to gather intelligence on anything that Sorge might consider to be pertinent to Soviet interests. If there was a particular piece of information he felt might help the USSR, it should be sent back.

There was already at least three intelligence groups working in Shanghai by the time Sorge arrived. Weingarten introduced a member of one, Max Clausen, who he had worked with previously in Hamburg. Clausen's abilities as a radio operator were made available to Sorge and his team as a matter of necessity. For particularly taxing jobs, they could call in Clausen and rely on his assistance in other matters. Radio technicians were, at the time, incredibly important to intelligence work. The ability to convey messages quickly and securely was a talent not possessed by a wealth of people. A good radioman was of extreme value to any intelligence officer. Not only were both men members of the Red Army, but they had emerged from the same branch of the German Communist Party in Hamburg. To test Clausen's abilities, Sorge ran him through an oral examination and found that his subject was more than competent, thanks to his time in the German Signals Corps during the war. After their work in Shanghai, Clausen would become a key figure in future Sorge operations.

Setting up Shop

One of the first issues Sorge encountered centred on Clausen's living arrangements. Choosing an apartment block in which he could both live and work, Clausen rented two rooms on separate floors. Hoping to have his radio room stationed above his own flat, he instead found that they were a floor apart, separated by a Finnish widow and her small apartment. Clausen ventured upstairs and offered to switch his larger apartment for her own, even offering to pay the difference. Eventually, the two struck up a romantic relationship and Clausen moved in with the woman. Sorge, perturbed by this arrangement, sought to meet with the woman. While he was met with resistance when gently probing communist ideals to her, and finding her unsuitable for work as a member of the team, he did concede that she would not jeopardize the mission. However, he warned Clausen that his permission would be revoked and that Moscow would be informed at the first indication that her presence was interfering with the group's 'secret work.' The woman – Anna – would eventually figure out the reason for Clausen's secret trips out and his obsession with radio, but she would remain with her husband.

Despite providing his permission for Clausen to remain with Anna, The radioman was soon moved away and dispatched to Manchuria to carry out work there. For this move, Sorge gave no reason. However, he had a capable operator in the form of Weingarten and Richard Sorge was soon moving across the town, introducing himself to various members of the international community. The intelligence and information he craved was known only to a few important people, so these were the people to whom he introduced himself. Carrying a letter of introduction provided by the German magazine, Grain, he positioned himself as a journalist writing articles on nutrition and agriculture in China.

One of his first targets was a man named Lieutenant Colonel Hermann von Kreibel, who worked as a military advisor to the government in Nanking, in good standing with Chiang Kai-shek's team of advisors. After integrating himself into the local society, Sorge found himself in high demand. To the locals, his cover story was slightly different. His high standard of English meant that he could pose as an American journalist. This allowed him to travel widely around China and to put together a burgeoning ring of enthusiastic workers. However, not everyone could be convinced by the American act. To a woman named Agnes Smedley, he knew that he would not be able to convince an American journalist that they shared the same nationality.

Agnes Smedley was the only contact who Sorge knew before he arrived in Shanghai. He had been told that he could depend on her assistance. She would prove to be key in the selection of Chinese workers whom Sorge hired. In fact, he was so pleased with her work that he suggested to the Comintern that she be recruited herself and put his name forward as one of the two sponsors required to join. While Agnes Smedley may have never been a member of any communist party, she was on Moscow's list of trusted persons. Smedley was a proven intellectual and a key cog in Sorge's espionage machine, but he later confessed to not finding her sexually attractive. Rather, he respected her abilities as an agent and knowing her allowed him to gain access to all of the most important left leaning social circles in Shanghai.

A Change of Focus

But as Sorge fell deeper and deeper into his mission, he soon discovered that he was unsatisfied with what Shanghai and China had to offer. If he was to truly understand what Asia was about, and how it pertained to Soviet Russia, then he would need to focus on the area's most dominant political power. While China may well have been the biggest nation in the area, there was a sensation emerging in Sorge's mind that if he was to ever understand the region, he would need to understand Japan. In response to this, he turned to Agnes Smedley and relied upon her social contacts and knack for tracking down exactly the right person for exactly the right job. If he was to fill in the repugnant gaps in his knowledge, then Sorge would need to acquaint himself with a Japanese national. It was this pursuit – and an introduction from Smedley – that soon led him to a man named Hotzumi Ozaki in the autumn months of 1930.

When they met, Richard Sorge felt an immediate bond with Hotzumi Ozaki. They shared similar faces and similar eyes; amicable, but belying a deeper working intelligence, with an underlying sense of coldness that permeated those who stared too long. Both men were known to indulge in their penchant for heavy drinking and both shared a long list of sexual conquests, women whom they would discuss with relish and enthusiasm. Both could speak English and German fluently, with Ozaki even speaking a small amount of Russian. Though Ozaki could read and write flawlessly in Chinese, his spoken language skills were still lacking. Despite this, they were a notable improvement over Sorge's own abilities.

Ozaki himself had emerged from a poor rural background, the son of parents who had been originally descended from the stock of rural samurais. Like Sorge, he had left his country of birth as a mere child when his parents had moved to Taiwan. He returned to Japan to attend university, after being taught Chinese by his father, who had become a successful newspaper editor in chief. Ozaki studied political science, just like Sorge. He began to develop communist sympathies throughout the 1920s, as well as falling into an unrequited romantic entanglement and a confounding set of government employment entrance exams. Eventually finding himself unmarried and without the government job he had wanted, he turned instead to journalism and newspaper work. Failing to report the news very well, he was instead transferred to a magazine department, where Ozaki began to flourish as the overseer of other people's stories. He wrote commentary and interpretation articles and built himself a studied enclave from which he was able to deconstruct and criticise others. He even married a girl from his childhood, though was far from the best example of a husband.

Despite the wealth of materials he had read, Ozaki did not enter into his marriage as a communist. The literature he had devoured had certainly been enjoyed, but he found himself unwilling to commit. He reluctantly attended a number of left-leaning political gatherings, as well as joining a local workers union under a false name. This proved to be a dangerous move when, in 1928, the Japanese police began to round up any suspected communists. Though he escaped their grasp, many of his friends were swept up in the operation. Those who were taken into custody were beaten and tortured, causing a great deal of disillusionment in Ozaki with regards to his home country. Just a few months later, he put in a request for a transfer and found himself working from the magazine's Shanghai department.

Having fled his homeland, Ozaki had noticed the growing signs of repression seeping into the culture. A growing military control over the government was echoed by the failures in suffrage and the inability to enact a truly democratic approach to governance. Despite the relative liberalism Ozaki had enjoyed during his time as a student, this version of Japan was rapidly disappearing. The appearance of a loosened, relaxed society after the First World War was simply an aesthetic change. But all attempts to turn to communism meant a known association with Russia, a long standing enemy of Japan. It soon became a criminal act to advocate for changes in the political system or to suggest the abolition of the concept of private property. This legislature was used to justify the arrest and detention of many communists or communist sympathizers.

The Great Depression of 1927 also had a huge impact on Japan, with those in charge beginning to view the previous decade's move towards more Western ideals as symptomatic of their problems. In an effort to jump start the economy, attempts were made to add power to the state rather than helping the individual citizens. Social restrictions grew stricter and censorship took hold of most of the media. Serious violations of the laws outlining communism could now result in death.

Ozaki arrived in Shanghai to discover that his previous notions about imperialist exploiters were incorrect. While he had correctly assumed the local workers to be mistreated and disenfranchised by the imperialist powers, he had assumed it would be the British who were chiefly at fault. Instead, it was Japan. If there were any leftist demonstrations in China, they were directed at his homeland, rather than the imperial powers he had assumed to be the key perpetrators. This fed into his guilty feelings about a privileged childhood in Japan-controlled Taiwan and altered his world view. Reading his copies of Marxist literature, Ozaki saw that events in China were following the exact patterns that had been established many years earlier. Rather than simply empathizing with the plight of the workers, Ozaki saw this adherence to Marxist formula as being indicative of its correct analysis. As such, he began to consider himself increasingly in agreement with Marxist principles. Such a person was easily malleable prey for Richard Sorge, who sprang upon Ozaki's leftist sympathies and nurtured them into fruition.

The relationship shared by Sorge and Ozaki would, in time, produce the best and most accurate intelligence that Richard Sorge received from any Japanese agent or source. In particular, the information he received regarding the Japanese government's new policy in Manchuria (their name for China) meant that he had solid data about how this policy would affect the USSR. This was exactly what Sorge's superiors wanted. Ozaki would be the portal through which Sorge introduced himself to the world of Chinese-Japanese relations, as well as the source of a huge amount of otherwise unobtainable information regarding these developments. With Japanese expansion in the Pacific a growing concern for Moscow, this began to take precedence over the local information Sorge was able to gather in China.

As well as this, Ozaki's early relationship with Sorge in Shanghai proved him to be a valuable asset in terms of recruiting. Once he had been convinced of the importance and power of a Communist state, Ozaki was able to turn his new found enthusiasm towards recruiting new agents. Several of the people Ozaki brought to Sorge in Shanghai would later be valuable agents in Japan. Ozaki did fall foul of a police visit from the Japanese consulate when he was found to have set up a small study group for Marxist literature at a local college. Though he spent ten days in jail – usually enough of an association to bar him from any kind of future espionage work – he continued to work for Sorge as a collector of military and political intelligence. He was again arrested and eventually deported; however, thus ending his association in Shanghai with Richard Sorge.

Leaving China

One of the agents Ozaki had brought into Sorge's circle was Teikichi Kawai and he proved to be a more than capable agent. Already able to cultivate and analyse data gathered from both the military and political institutions, his position as a Japanese newspaper worker in Shanghai provided Kawai with a good cover story and good access to information. When he first met Sorge, Ozaki was there to function as an interpreter, but the bond of trust between the two grew and Kawai was soon recruited and made into a fine agent for Sorge's circle. Kawai's first mission was to collect any information about any Japanese military activity in North China, close to the Russian border. He was told not to rush things and Sorge implored him to take the work step by step.

These words remained with the young Japanese man, who had been impressed by the fascinating, electrically charged character Richard Sorge conveyed during their first meeting. Originally a communist for pacifistic reasons, Kawai was not a conventional leftist. Drawn to China after graduating from university, he joined his local communist party once abroad and this was where he met Ozaki. After being persuaded to cut ties with the other organisations to better preserve his cover, he was welcomed into the ever expanding circle of Sorge's intelligence network.

But after the deportation of Hotzumi Ozaki, Richard Sorge became increasingly disillusioned with the intelligence gathering mission he had founded in Shanghai. His efforts in this respect are not the most noteworthy or most dangerous of his career. Instead, it became the breeding ground for his future role as the greatest spy the world has ever seen. It was here, in 1920s China, that Sorge refined the techniques he would use to grow an intelligence organization out of the ground. It was here that he met key players in his future missions. It was here, with relatively little on the line in terms of existential threats, that he was freer to work on his craft without the threat of imminent death. All of the ground we have covered to this point – rather than revealing Sorge as the amazing spy he was – has simply laid the foundations for the daring do of his later missions. Once he was free of China and Shanghai, Sorge's obsession with the Asian arena would lead him to the increasingly paranoid Japan in order to construct one of the most important spy networks in all of human history.

The Next Steps

Richard Sorge's initial mission in Shanghai had originally been planned for two years. The difficulty of the entire process led to the Fourth Department keeping him in China for an additional year, but he was recalled to Moscow in 1932. After a short while, it was decided that Sorge should pursue his interests in Japan. But cracking open the nut of Imperial Japan would not prove to be easy. Unlike in China, his cover story would need to become even more watertight. Japan was renowned as one of the most powerful and paranoid nations in the world. With the death penalty for suspected communists already in place, the discovery of a Soviet spy would lead to far worse treatment. In order to prevent such an uncovering from taking place, Sorge would need to tighten his cover. To do this, he would need to travel back to Germany and secure his credentials at every level. With the Germany of 1933 in the midst of a political take over by Adolf Hitler, the sudden rule of the Nazi party presented a challenge all of its own. If Sorge wanted to spy in Imperial Japan, he would first need to navigate the increasingly tortuous waters of Nazi Germany.

The Rise of Japan

On return from China, Sorge was met with a warm reception. His work in Shanghai had produced a great deal of useful intelligence and he was met by General Berzin, the head of the Fourth Department. They described their agent's work as 'most satisfactory' and began to plot how best to use his skills in their goal to infiltrate governments across the world using their intelligence network. While Sorge had floated the idea that he might be given a position in Moscow from which he could oversee operations, Berzin and his associates agreed that Sorge was much more useful in the field. After such exemplary work, however, they conceded that he might be allowed to remain in Russia until he had written a book about his knowledge of Chinese agriculture.

Another reason for Sorge's apparent desire to stay in Russia was the appearance of a woman known across the country as Mrs Sorge. This woman, Yekaterina Alexandrovna – Katcha for short – was seemingly the woman who he intended to marry. Nine years younger than her potential husband, she was a former drama student at Leningrad who had left her studies behind and worked in a factory. She had helped Sorge perfect his Russian, though the couple had not spent too much time together. A few weeks here, a few months there – the relationship seemed strained, to say the least. Even before Sorge had completed his book, the couple had briefly separated, but would variously be engaged and, later, married. Talking to Berzin on the phone, Sorge seemed eager to prove himself once more, but was forced to swallow his disappointment at the news that he would not be granted any more time for his writing. When asked where he would like to be stationed, Sorge deliberated a short while before suggesting – half joking – that Tokyo 'is not bad!' He had assumed a post in Japan would be considered outside the realms of what any agent could achieve, or at least, what Moscow was willing to sanction.

Berzin did not commit to the idea at first – Japan seemed almost impenetrable, even for one of their best agents – but soon came around to the idea. Sorge seemed convinced that this sudden interest came from much higher up the food chain, potentially interesting the man now cemented as leader of the Soviet Union, Joseph Stalin. They began to plot how Sorge might go about his new mission.

Tokyo, it seems, was an increasingly legitimate target. The Soviets had increasing reasons to suspect Japan and to feel threatened by the nation's activities. The Japanese policy of expansion in the Pacific had been in place since the turn of the century. Already, Russia had joined diplomatic efforts to France and Germany in an attempt to convince Japan to return the Liaotung peninsula to China. Added to this, the war between Japan and Russia in 1905 – focused on ownership of Korea –

had worried the Russians, especially due to the manner in which the Japanese were able to decimate the Russian navy. Russia had been forced to concede Korea, as well as half of Sakhalin Island. Japan's limited involvement in the First World War had left them with a thriving economy and control of many of the formerly German colonies in the Pacific arena. During the Russian civil war, in the wake of the Bolshevik Revolution, Japan had joined the USA in committing a large number of troops and had wrested control of large tracts of land.

Now, both countries were looking at Manchuria. Manchuria was the name given to a huge area of China in the north of the country. A secret meeting in 1907 had divided the country into several different spheres of influence, but the Japanese felt they had been short changed by the deal. Large deposits of coal and iron in the region made it a particularly rewarding target and these were resources Japan was sorely lacking.

The issue came to a head when members of the Kwantung Army (a Japanese group station in China) demolished a bridge in the region and blamed it on the Chinese. The Japanese were quick to act – in what they claimed was a retaliatory move – and occupied the city of Mukden. Now known as the Mukden incident, the situation rapidly expanded into the Manchurian incident and, soon, a full invasion of China was underway and Japan controlled almost all of the territory north of the Great Wall. This was right along the border of the newly-formed Soviet Union and the Russians had little reason to believe that the Japanese were happy with just this much. The two countries feared one another's potential and both were suspicious of the other's intentions. As such, it seemed important for Sorge to uncover as much information as possible about the goals of the Imperial Japanese.

Forming a Plan

The Fourth Department agreed that Richard Sorge should spent the next two years attempting to erect a spy network in Japan. His mission was given four questions, with his goal being to find the answer to the following:

- Would Sorge and his fellow Russians be able to gain legal access to Japan?
- Was it really possible – as foreigners – to communicate with the native Japanese people?
- Was it possible to establish radio communications between Japan and the Soviet mainland?
- Could Sorge and his agents collect intelligence regarding Japan's intentions towards Russia?

Sorge was to return after two years of trying to find the answers, if he had lived to tell the tale. A special cipher was developed for the mission, using the German Statistical Yearbook (1933 Edition) as a basis. This hinted at the plan for Sorge's cover. He would pose again as a German reporter, with the agent cultivating the idea that he was an intrepid, dashing, committed reporter of German news. Because he would stand out among the locals and was a memorable figure regardless, he would embrace his idiosyncrasies. Rather than try to blend in, he would deliberately stand out. He would be entirely unable to pose as an American as he had in Shanghai – many of the top Japanese officials whom he wished to befriend spoke better English than he did. Instead, he was to ingratiate himself with the German embassy in Tokyo. He would need a position at a high ranking German paper and credentials of the highest quality from Germany. This presented perhaps the biggest problem.

It is hard to think of a worse time for a Soviet agent to attempt to infiltrate the burgeoning Third Reich. Hitler's election as chancellor in 1933 had given him unprecedented control over the Weimar government of the post-War years. After only a few days in the position, one of the Fuhrer's first moves had been to declare communism illegal. This was not without precedent, as his SA forces had a long history of attacking, beating, and even killing various members of the German Communist parties. The Nazis banned communism, shut down its papers, attacked party members, and sent members of the left to the early iterations of the concentration camps. Hitler considered the Bolshevik Revolution to be controlled by an unseen Jewish influence and positioned the ideology as one of several state-specified targets of hatred. Accordingly, many of Sorge's old comrades had fled, been imprisoned, or had resigned their beliefs. For a man with a long history in the various communist organizations of Germany, the Third Reich was one of the most dangerous places in the world. But Richard Sorge needed German documentation. He found himself, in May of 1933, moving ever closer to the borders of Germany, taking the first steps towards his mission in Tokyo.

Into the Belly of the Beast

Richard Sorge was still a German citizen and his papers were still very much intact. There did exist a 'watchlist' at German border outposts, indicating to the guards which people they might want to be wary of, but Sorge happened to not be included among the names. A common feature in Sorge's life, he fortunately managed to get through the check without arousing suspicion, despite his years of communist activism in Germany. After this, he made his way to Berlin, the city where he had spent the majority of his youth and the headquarters of the rising Nazi powers.

Swastikas were everywhere to be found. They hung from every building and adorned the arm of every soldier in the street. There was an atmosphere of war, even if the leader was still preaching peace. Courageous and filled with self-confidence, Richard Sorge moved through the city as though nothing posed a threat. His experiences in Shanghai, as well as secretly assisting the Soviet Union, had established Sorge's credentials as an actual reporter. This gave him a head start as he sought out journalism jobs. According to Sorge, he found work with the Frankfurter Zeitung as a Japanese correspondent, thanks to a reference he received from colleagues such as Hede Massing. The paper denies this, however, suggesting that they only heard from Sorge for the first time in 1936. With their reputation to protect, as well as Sorge's history of indulging his flights of fancy, it's hard to discern the truth.

What is more likely, however, is Sorge's story about how he met up with a representative from the Comintern in Berlin. The unnamed man met with Sorge in a café, whereupon they exchanged code words, and sat down to hold a conversation in German, pretending to be old war associates. They exchanged information and allowed for Sorge to check in with his superiors. Such a meeting demonstrates that, while Sorge's efforts to enter into Germany were dangerous and fraught with peril, he was not the sole communist agent working at the time. But with his history as a party member in Nazi Germany, he was certainly more at risk than one might expect.

However, Sorge still chased down leads and endeavored to make things happen. He needed further contacts and decided to call upon the offices of the German Journal of Geopolitics. They were well respected among the Nazis and would provide Sorge with a means of rubber stamping his credentials throughout Germany. The editor was a man named Kurt Vowinckel, who was well regarded as both a publisher and one of Hitler's most fervent supporters. He had also read the essays Sorge had published on Chinese agriculture and, as luck would have it, was finally pleased to be able to meet the writer. Vowinckel asked Sorge to contribute articles to his own publication, and the Soviet spy was more than happy to accept. This provided him not only with a pretext for being in Japan, but the well-regarded author also wrote a letter of introduction. This could be presented to Germans in Tokyo to establish Sorge's credentials. It could be presented at the German Embassy, for example, in order to ingratiate the spy with the local German community and dissuade any suspicion that he might be anything other than what he claimed. While people might still suspect him to be a spy, they would likely assume that he was working for the Nazis rather than the Soviets. This key distinction was an example of the natural audacity and cunning Sorge exercised in his work. Sorge spent the next few weeks travelling around Germany and building up his reputation as a German of some standing and a bona fide Nazi. He introduced himself to numerous high-ranking academics and writers, who in turn would lend credence to his cover story. Despite the volatile, hostile nature of his surroundings, Sorge was able to foil his way into many German inner circles.

One of the men he met was a Munich professor named Dr. Karl Haushofer, who had been one of the founding members of the Journal of Geopolitics. Haushofer's reputation as a professor and author lent him authority across the country. As well as this, he had been part of an army unit that had served in Japan before the war and had produced a huge amount of writing about the country and the culture. It was his opinion that the Japanese people would inevitably rule over all of Asia. His highly placed Nazi contacts and his friendship with Rudolf Hess (deputy Fuhrer) dated back decades, including writing a book about Japan together regarding the subject of espionage. Just like the Japanese, the Germans hoped to learn from fellow countrymen who were living abroad, going so far as to establish cells of agents during the 1930s. Hess was eventually placed at the head of the Foreign Department in Nazi Germany, which oversaw this kind of operations, keeping track of every card-carrying Nazi around the globe. Through the association with Hess, the approval of Haushofer would provide a huge amount of credibility for Sorge's cover story. Accordingly, he received a letter of introduction to the ambassador from Germany to Japan, as well as one to Japan's ambassador to the USA.

These letters acted as a seal of approval for Richard Sorge. If his story as a convincing German journalist was to be believed, the more letters he could acquire, the better. It was seemingly impossible that a Soviet agent might be able to infiltrate the German political and academic ranks so successfully. Thanks to the sheer outlandish nature of his plan and the high regard in which his articles on China were held, Sorge succeeded. His intellectual capacity as a writer meant that the work he had produced on China was incredibly well regarded. Editors were more than happy to commission work from him, as all he asked in exchange was a simple reference that he might make introductions to the local German community when he arrived in Tokyo. Such letters also arrived from Dr. Zeller, editor of the slightly anti-Nazi paper named Tuglische Rundschau (which would soon be abolished), who introduced Sorge to both the embassy in Tokyo and, most importantly, to a man named Lieutenant Colonel Eugen Ott. Ott worked as the exchange officer in Nagoya with one of Japan's artillery regiments. Zeller, truly believing in Sorge, stressed that Ott was to trust in absolutely everything Sorge said to him. Not only was this a letter of introduction, but it went much further, imploring the recipient to trust the holder "politically, personally, and otherwise."

For any German living abroad, the rise of Hitler had meant an inherent suspicion of anyone who might try to befriend them. Dr. Zeller's letter neatly sidestepped this issue and provided Sorge with more than just politically influential contacts. At the time, however, Sorge was unaware just how important a role the letter would play. Rather than merely exchange officers, his targets were considerably more powerful. Such was the nature of the German Embassy that any contact Sorge could make was well worth his effort. This would allow him to cultivate information not only about Japan, but about Germany as well. Feeding all of the intelligence up the food chain to the Soviet High Command, Sorge's position as a German writer in Japan provided him with intelligence from two sources at the same time. During this preliminary stage, Sorge was still supremely confident, and his writings from the time show no indication that he might have allowed doubt to enter his mind.

But there was one key element to the plan that Sorge alone would have to put into practice. He would have to be accepted as a Nazi. Thanks to the then-current political climate in Germany, anyone of any importance needed to be a paid-up member of the party if they were to be trusted or allowed to prosper. If Richard Sorge was to convince people that he was a German abroad, he would need to convince them that he was, in fact, a national socialist.

In order to accomplish this, Sorge acquired huge amounts of Nazi literature and propaganda. He memorized the slogans and key phrases. He mimicked the gestures. He poured through Hitler's own book, *Mein Kampf*, with particular care. In an eerie echo of his first forays into communist literature during his months recovering in a field hospital, the Soviet spy devoured the Nazi culture in order to better present himself as a fully convincing member.

It was not long before he could be found putting his newly learned words into practice. He could shout, scream, and argue with the fellow party members. He was able to recite full passages of *Mein Kampf* off the top of his head. The friends he met as part of his forays into the Nazi party began to take him to that old German favorite, the beer hall. So often was he attending these alcohol-laden functions that Sorge – despite being a committed heavy drinker – was forced to give up drinking, lest he lose his senses and let slip a clue as to his real intentions. He described this new teetotal approach as "the bravest thing I ever did." Despite the confidence and the audacity that he had exhibited thus far, the commitment to giving up one of his favorite past times (and a key part of the German culture he was attempting to ingratiate himself into) demonstrated the fine line between extraordinary success and terrible failure that this mission presented. One drunken slip of the tongue in 1933 Berlin, and he might as well be signing his own death sentence.

Once he was confident in his ability to present himself as a Nazi, Sorge began the process of applying to become a member of the party. Newspaper correspondents at the time were required to be members, seeing as the state controlled the media. In order to succeed, Sorge presented himself via the approval of a number of the editors to whom he had recently been talking. Despite this referral system, the process of approval also dictated a background check, performed by the Gestapo, the Nazi's secret police. Despite the communist activities in his earlier life, Sorge's confident projection of a Nazi persona was seemingly enough. Thanks to his hard work and likely a little bit of luck, he was accepted. Richard Sorge was provided with a membership card, though it would not reach him until a number of months later, by which time he was already in Japan.

Sorge's approval was indeed a lucky event. His extensive history as a communist in Germany would typically have prevented him from being approved, but – as Douglas MacArthur has suggested – the power of the Gestapo in 1933 was not quite as extensive and as all-encompassing as we might typically assume. Though they would later evolve into a comprehensive national network, the secret police were not as yet quite as efficient. Also, MacArthur has suggested that there might well have been a Soviet spy present in the approvals offices who purposely ignored the history of communist activity. When the same check was performed in 1941, Sorge's extensive left-leaning political career came immediately to light.

The suggestion of an agent on the inside of the membership process was all but confirmed by Hede Massing, who later wrote that there was a "guardian angel" watching over Sorge's application process. Sorge was aware of this agent, though never knew him by name. He was indebted to the undercover Gestapo worker, however, who had removed all of the incriminating evidence at just the right moment. In July of 1933, now armed with many letters of recommendation and being an official member of the Nazi party, Richard Sorge was ready to begin his mission. He picked up a German passport and began to travel west. First to France and England, and then on to New York.

Sorge stayed a short while in America, at the Lincoln Hotel in New York City. While it is not entirely clear what he did during his fifteen-day stopover, Sorge himself suggested that he met a man he didn't know, who put him in contact with an operative from the Washington Post, meeting the man at the World's Fair in Chicago. Next, Sorge travelled to Washington and began to move west once more. He stopped in Chicago to meet his fellow agent and received information on how he could contact the Japanese assistant who he had requested during the mission's planning stages. It was important to Sorge that the assistant be Japanese with a strong command of English. In order to find this person, he was to place an ad in the Japan Advertiser once he arrived in his destination. The ad would ask for the purchase of Ukiyoe, a specific variety of print from Japan. His new assistant would be the person to reply. His next stop was in Vancouver, where he went aboard a ship named the Empress of Russia and began to cross over, at last, into Japan. Now fully embroiled in his ideological disguise, Sorge was on the verge of his most dangerous mission yet.

A Dangerous Game

In Japan, Richard Sorge found himself in an entirely alien society. Without a grasp of the language, his first forays into Tokyo high society were filled with dangers. Armed only with his Nazi credentials and his perpetual self-confidence, he was charged with establishing a nascent spy ring, and for the first time in Soviet history, constructing an intelligence network spanning German and Japanese intelligence at the same time. This required him to be spying on two of the world's most paranoid states simultaneously. The work he would carry out over the coming years would cement Sorge's position as the greatest spy who ever lived. But it would not be easy.

Making Introductions

With his letters of introduction in hand, Sorge began to make waves in Japan. He introduced himself to officials at the German Embassy, as well as representatives from the Japanese Foreign Ministry. His abundance of connections impressed the locals, who in turn began to introduce him to other members of various social circles gathering in Tokyo in 1933. At times like these, Sorge was in his element. A social, enrapturing man, he could charm anyone. His wit and intellect endeared him to almost everyone he met. This was purposeful. One of Sorge's first objectives was to become close with members of the German Embassy staff. The "absolute trust" he earned from the staff members would, in his own words, form the "foundation of [Sorge's] spy activity in Japan." The extent to which this Soviet spy ingratiated himself in the German foreign embassy is an achievement that Sorge himself claims has "no equivalent in history."

Sorge spent his first few months in Japan familiarizing himself with his new surroundings. He worked hard to build up a network of friends and social acquaintances, all the while studying the minutia of the local culture. But in addition to this, he needed to maintain his cover story. This meant writing. His first political essay was very well received in Germany. So much so that the staff at the German embassy began to respect Sorge for his insight and journalistic skills. Among these, a man named Josef Knoll became a key point of interest for the spy. As commercial secretary for the Embassy, he was "number one in terms of political knowledge among the Germans. Knoll would become a key contact.

Everything seemed to point towards a tightening of military and political ties between Germany and Japan. This, of course, posed a serious threat to the Soviet Union. The appointment of Herbert von Dirksen as envoy to Japan was indicative of this slight change in direction and the man proved to be a difficult issue for Sorge. A committed Prussian military man, he accepted Sorge for his journalist credentials but was seemingly impossible to draw close. Sorge had very little to offer Dirksen, so Dirksen was more than content to keep the supposed journalist at arm's length. If Sorge was to gain insight into the Embassy's intelligence, then approaching the man at the very top seemed impossible.

Another important introduction demanded a trip to Nagoya. Eugen Ott was the liaison officer for a Japanese artillery regiment. His job was to live on base and to feed information back regarding the training regimes of the local armed forces, usually conducted in top secret. Sorge had a letter written to Ott suggesting that the military man place his full confidence and trust in the letter bearer. This was made easy thanks to Sorge's growing Japanese skills, which – while not brilliant- were far greater than Ott's and allowed the German soldier someone in whom he could confide.

Ott was lucky enough to avoid the Nazi purges of 1934. During his early military career, he had allied himself to the wrong man. After making his allegiance known to Hitler, the higher-ups in the German

Army had conspired to stash him out of the way in order to avoid the Fuhrer's wrath. As a result, Ott was sent to Japan, almost as far away from the Third Reich as was possible. When Hitler began a process of culling his political rivals and undesirables, Ott's favored commander was one of the first to fall victim to the Night of the Long Knives. All the way out in Japan, Ott avoided the fate suffered by so many of his compatriots in one of the worst of Hitler's purges. The episode left Ott with little love for Adolf Hitler, though he was certainly a patriotic man. He and Sorge shared a history in the Germany army of World War I and were able to bond over their experiences. They also had a shared love of chess. Ott would be promoted in 1934 and would move to Tokyo to become a military attaché at the embassy. In another stroke of good fortune, Sorge already enjoyed the man's confidence as he moved upwards through the ranks.

The position Ott would move into was hugely important for Sorge's spy ring. As military attaché, he evaluated everything the Germans had learned through their close relationship with the Japanese and through their own espionage efforts. Ott looked over all of this and sent it back to Berlin. Soon, he came to rely on Sorge as a sounding board for information and as a provider of advice and good judgement. Ott's work included information about Japan, as well as information regarding Germany's plans as they pertained to the Far East. Through this one relationship, Sorge was able to discover a huge amount about German military activity, as well as the German intelligence about the Japanese, and feed it back to his Soviet commanders.

Entering into Tokyo's German community was, for Sorge, easy enough. At the time of his arrival, the community numbered close to a thousand families – something like a small village. As a personable man with contacts at the embassy, he had no trouble inserting himself into the community in a convincing fashion. Everyone appeared to consider him a top-rate though slightly eccentric journalist; one who was slightly apolitical, neither a strict Nazi nor communist sympathizer.

The final part of the puzzle was to ratify his journalistic credentials. This, Sorge achieved in a similar fashion. Networking among the most prominent German journalists in the area, he soon befriended people such as Rudolf Weise, who was head of the official German News Bureau. As well as the professional connections, Sorge's relationship with Weise was such that the man might occasionally pass along titbits of gossip. All of the information was accumulated and sent back to the USSR.

Richard Sorge cultivated the image of a slightly lazy, slightly whimsical, though incredibly adept journalist. Rather than our traditional image of a spy working in utter secrecy, he projected a gossipy, intellectual persona with watertight credentials. It was almost impossible to doubt his position and seemingly incredulous that he might be any kind of spy, especially for the USSR. So tight were his connections to the German Embassy that the Japanese would assume him to be a German agent (if at all) while the Germans considered him too ingratiated in German society to be anything less than what he claimed. Soon, after delving deeper into a study of Japan and its affairs, he became an expert on all matters relating to the country. Over the next decade, he would gather over a thousand books on the subject, even going so far as to commission translations of books he thought he should read. So deep into his cover did he seem, that when an opening for the head of the local Nazi organization appeared, he was urged by many to take the position. He declined, but continued to use the group to ascertain base level opinions as they rose up within the Nazi party.

Putting Together a Team

In order to make the most of the time spent gathering information in Tokyo, Sorge needed to put together a team. A great deal of this was handled by the Fourth Department, who approved candidates and set them up with Sorge in advance. While he was able to recruit many people for his network in Tokyo, a great deal of the work would be handled by the approved Marxists with whom he had been paired.

The first was a Croatian man named Branko de Voukelitch. He had fallen in and out of love with communism, but his writings on his time in the Yugoslavian army had convinced many in the organization of his ideological strength. He was to be the photographer for the group and would need to set up a dark room in his home. His first apartment was too small, so one of the first things he did in Tokyo was move to another.

Another key player was Bruno Wendt, a German Communist Party member who had spent time attending the Moscow Radio School. He would be responsible for broadcasting the group's findings back to base. He too would need to set up shop in his home but encountered a problem when the decoy business he had set up was based out of Yokohama rather than Tokyo. Assuming a cover as an exporter of Japanese sample products, he was in entirely the wrong city. For Sorge, this was a major inconvenience.

Sorge's assistant came to him exactly as Moscow had planned. Noticing an ad in the Japan Advertiser for Ukiyoe, a Japanese man named Miyagi responded. He set up a meeting with Voukelitch, who checked him out before Sorge agreed to meet. Miyagi met his future boss in the shadow of the Ueno Art Gallery, with both wearing color coordinated ties to identify one another. Sorge wore black while Miyagi wore blue. The two men shared a passion for art and would occasionally put aside their espionage to visit their favorite works.

These three men formed the basis of Sorge's operation, but he was not entirely happy. Wendt was a nervous and paranoid radioman. Voukelitch had little experience. Miyagi, while the best of the three, lacked the real conviction and made Sorge promise that – should a more suitable candidate be found – that he be replaced. By Sorge's reckoning, this rag tag group needed at least one more person: a native Japanese agent who had contacts in the highest political and social groups. He delved back into his past and one man stood out: Ozaki.

Ozaki had been sent back to Japan after his communist activity in China. Now working on the foreign section of a national newspaper, he had a family and was living in Osaka. But balanced delicately on the fence between disavowing his communist thinking and joining up to the party full time (a dangerous prospect in a nation turning against the left), Richard Sorge found his old friend in the perfect position to mold into one of the key figures in his growing intelligence network.

The Art of Spying

Many people have debated Ozaki's role in the spy network. He was not as drawn into the espionage trade when compared to many of the people with whom Sorge was working. For example, Sorge was happy to allow the Japanese man to continue to call him the code name he had labored under while in Japan – Johnson – for two years. It was only by accident that Ozaki came across Sorge's real name. However, the Soviet spy did put Ozaki's name forward to the Comintern and sponsored his membership. Of the two major powers in the region, Ozaki saw Japan rather than Russia as the likely aggressor in any eventual war. He decided to help the spies in order to save as many Japanese lives as possible. While some have suggested that he simply supplied information to Sorge that he came across, others have indicated that Ozaki was involved in more complicated espionage work of his own.

This idea is certainly borne out by the lecture Ozaki delivered once on the art of spying. When examining his key thoughts about the craft, it is possible to see how far he was willing to go once he was a member of Sorge's team.

He included the points:

- A spy should never act as though they are eager to hear any news. It belies the cautious and reluctant nature of many people at the time.
- It is possible to encourage people to reveal information by convincing them that the spy knows more than he actually does. Discussing shared knowledge is easier than revealing new information.

- It is possible to receive general hints by listening closely at those parties and social events where people are drinking, but have not yet gotten too wild.
- Being an expert in a certain field means people will come to the spy of their own free will. Ozaki, for example, was an expert on China and would answer questions and queries from curious people. Information could be learned through these inquiries without anyone realizing.
- A role in the news and media means that information gathering (both direct and indirect) is simply part of the job and an excellent cover story.
- Local opinions can be gathered by attending talks and lectures in rural areas. Frequent attendance can be used to gauge public opinion.
- It is possible to achieve a natural relationship with the best contacts simple by establishing direct relationships with important sources of information.
- The real secret to espionage is to win the confidence of others and to arrange for personal conditions where the exchange of information between the two parties is simply natural.

These secrets were likely lifted directly from Sorge or from observing the way in which he operated. While Sorge left us nothing similar, Ozaki's lecture on the matter can give insight into how Sorge went about setting up his spy network. We have already begun to notice the building of relationships and the winning of other people's confidence. With the seeds of social activity already sewn, it would simply be a matter of time before Sorge was able to start harvesting the information.

When Ozaki was recruited by Sorge, however, he agreed to take part in the operation with one resounding warning. Japan was an entirely different beast to Shanghai. The casual nature of the Chinese city contrasted heavily with the discipline of the Japanese capital. The police here were stricter by many orders of magnitude. This came as no surprise to the Soviet spy, who knew all previous attempts by the USSR to lay down a spy network in the country had failed.

A Mutual Benefit

While it appears that Sorge's employ of his various agents was simply a one-way street, the relationship was often mutually beneficial. For example, the career of Eugen Ott was boosted considerably by his association with Sorge. He would pass on information and, in return, receive access to Sorge's host of Japanese contacts, to his sharp analysis, and to an insight into Japanese culture he might never have managed. Before long, he was Dirksen's most valued advisor and spoke with the Embassy leader on many topics.

Meanwhile, Ozaki transferred his newspaper position to Tokyo. In doing so, the publication requested that he become involved with a research branch known as the East Asia Problems Investigation Association. The department was designed to bring together many of the smartest analysts in Japan to survey issues from across Asia. As an expert on China, Ozaki was now able to pick the brains of leaders on matters such as the government, the army, the navy, and the Foreign Ministry, all of whom had representatives or experts on the board. The insight was incredible not only in a professional sense for Ozaki, but it also supplied Sorge with access to classified and important materials. Likewise, through Sorge, Ozaki managed to perfect his knowledge of matters of Europe and areas outside of Asia. Shortly, Ozaki was one of the foremost experts on life outside of Japan and his expertise was highly valued.

Sorge worked to interweave relationships such as these. He might pass on information and insight from Ozaki to Ott, who would then convey it to Dirksen. Having gratefully discussed these problems, the German attaché was more than willing to share other information, which Sorge could then pass back to Ozaki and complete the circle. The two agents didn't come into contact with each other. Rather, Sorge was the conduit through which all of the information passed. He supplemented this with the intelligence Voukelitch was acquiring from other Europeans and Americans and soon found himself sitting on a gold mine of data.

After the First Year

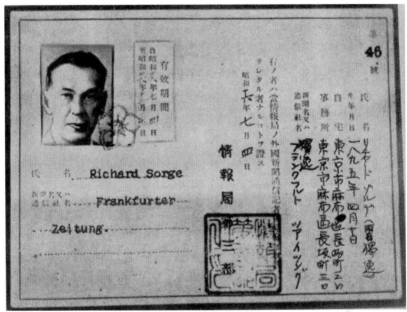

Richard Sorge Press Pass

Having spent his first twelve months in Tokyo constructing a network of spies, Sorge now went about the business of reporting his findings to Moscow. He gathered together the information from the sources, condensed into its purest form, and added his own touches as an editorialist. These reports were highly valued in the Soviet Union, and Sorge's satisfaction showed. His network was growing stronger, though they never met together. Sorge would visit each of his three main sources – Ott, Ozaki, and Voukelitch – individually and talk with them alone. He would read through Miyagi's translations and codify everything before sending it to Wendt to radio back to Russia. Only he would know the final content of the messages before it was decrypted back at the Fourth Department.

The network was something like a spider, with the legs reaching out in various directions. Sorge was the body of the arachnid, while each new source was another leg. He controlled their ongoing search and saw all of the information they brought to him. After a year in Tokyo, Sorge's intelligence network was only starting to show its true value.

Big Changes

The network was never static. For example, the disintegration of Voukelitch's marriage was met by Moscow with the news that he should divorce his wife and marry a Japanese woman in order to bring him close to the native community. He joined the French news organization Havas, and his work as a photographer had a greater set of credentials than ever before. He now had an excuse to be out photographing all kinds of public figures and had fallen deeply in love with a Japanese girl.

Of all the various elements of Sorge's spy ring, only one was giving him real trouble. Wendt, the radioman, was a slow worker with a paranoid mindset. Sorge saw him as incompetent and a threat to the operation. His inadequacies severely limited the amount of information Sorge could transmit to the USSR. With so much to think about, however, Sorge simply had to deal with his radio operative's failures.

Radio signals were vital. In the early days, a bulk of the information exchanges were handled by courier meetings. Sorge might visit a tourist spot with a package under his arm, spot another man with the same, and the two would share conversational code words. They would swap the packages and arrange for the next meeting. Inside the parcels, Sorge could send documents, microfilms, and other important pieces of information. He could receive cash and orders from his superiors. The radio was essential if these meetings were to be arranged or cancelled. Wendt's incompetence placed Sorge at even greater risk.

In the meantime, his successful journalism career and the huge amounts of research he was conducting meant that he was soon outgrowing the hotel room where he had stayed for the first twelve months. He acquired residence in a house on a small compound. It was particularly interesting to note the presence of a police station nearby, the view from which could see directly into Sorge's home. This was yet another element of the cover story. What self-respecting spy would live in a home in such blatant view of the authorities? While all foreigners were suspected of spying, this seemingly German journalist was apparently too outgoing and obvious to be anything like a secret agent. He was quizzed occasionally, but only as much as any other foreign national. Richard Sorge's cover was seemingly complete.

Sorge's daily routine, after twelve months, had been perfected. His new home was fairly untidy, with only a few paintings by Miyagi (whose cover story was a job as an artist) hanging on the walls. A few pieces of art and a lot of books were downstairs, while the upstairs was a mess. There was little that he could not drop in thirty seconds should he suddenly feel the need to leave. In response to this, Sorge hired a cleaning lady who soon inspired his utter respect. She would cook and clean for him each day, despite his seeming lack of interest in either, but would become a regular feature of his day. She arrived at five in the morning and began to run his bath. He would rise at six sharp, scrub himself clean, run through some brief exercises, and then dress in one of his expertly tailored outfits. Then, he would work at his typewriter furiously until it was time for lunch, after which he had an hour-long nap. The housekeeper departed at three in the afternoon, after which time he was able to engage in social activities or receive more espionage related guests. He gave her the nick name Ama-san, translating loosely into "honorable housekeeper" and reflected that she seemed to enjoy the position very much. Typically, his evenings would involve a small effort on a set of barbells before setting out into the town to discover what information he could in bars, cafes, and restaurants.

Bright Prospects

Having had a year to establish his spy network, the Fourth Department sent a call for him to come to Moscow in May of 1935. Sorge was keen to demonstrate what he had achieved so far, to seek permission to escalate his efforts, and to receive confirmation as to exactly what information the superiors might want to hear from his team. Travelling back to Moscow meant attempting to cover his tracks. Moving via America, he was furnished with a fake passport and an Australian visa. His own documents would not bear the marks of his journey. He tried to avoid a paper trail, slipping through the exit tax when boarding his ship. He was nearly caught by an official and asked to leave the boat, but a $50 bribe managed to get him out of trouble.

Despite the near brush with disaster, Sorge's confidence was evident. He carried with him all his materials, despite being explicitly told not to. On arrival in Moscow, he met with a man named Uritskii, who had succeeded Berzin as the head of the Fourth Department. In their discussions, Sorge revealed that establishing a spy ring in Japan was indeed possible. He gave a detailed report of his experiences and hinted towards the bright prospects he foresaw for the future. Uritskii's response seemed to reflect the organization's pleasure at Sorge's success and agreed that he would outline some areas of key interest, but granted Sorge permission to chase down information he thought most interesting. Tactical decisions would also be at the behest of the man on the ground, so long as they resulted in any information regarding the Soviet's key areas of interest. As told to Sorge, these were:

- Japan's intentions and policies as they pertained to the Soviet Union, especially any indications that an attack might be imminent. This was to be considered the number one priority.
- Any alterations or reorganizations of Japan's army and air units, especially those that might threaten Russia.
- The relationship between Germany and Japan.
- Japan's attitude and intentions with regards to China.
- Japan's relationship with the USA and Great Britain.

- Any information about the Japanese army, including the military's influence on the nation's politics.
- Heavy industry in Japan and how it was being developed.

Essentially, the Russians wanted to know whether Japan (either by themselves or with alliances) posed a threat to the USSR, and whether it possessed the power to accomplish such an attack. In return for uncovering such information, Sorge made three requests of his superiors. Firstly, he asked for Ozaki to be recognized as a key member of the intelligence network. Secondly, he requested that he be given free rein to conduct relationships with the German Embassy as he saw fit, potentially to dispel rumors that he might be drawing too close to the Nazi officials and, as such, could no longer be trusted. Finally, he requested a new radio operator. He suggested either Clausen or Weingarten replace Wendt, whose work was not satisfactory. Uritskii agreed to all three conditions.

Sorge was given his choice of either Weingarten or Clausen. Wendt had also travelled to Moscow and was on the spot to train his replacement. He had not been informed by Sorge that his work thus far was not satisfactory. Instead, he had needled Wendt's own fears and suggested to him that an exit from Japan was the safest option. Wendt agreed and travelled willingly. Sorge selected Clausen as the replacement and met him in a bar to explain his plan. Clausen had failed after being sent to Manchuria and was punished by the authorities with a reform through labor program. He and Anna were sent to a rural area, where Clausen worked on providing farmers with radio networks. It was a comfortable life, and he twice refused the order to return to Moscow. Shortly after being asked a third and final time, he found himself seated opposite Sorge as he learned about his return to the world of espionage.

Richard Sorge left Russia shortly after. He had little time during his visit to speak to friends or even the woman who he now regarded as his wife, at least in a legal sense. As he departed, he was now solely to answer to the Fourth Department. No other institution in the USSR held sway over his actions, not even Stalin himself. He said goodbye to friends and the city itself. It would be the last time he ever laid foot on Russian soil. His wife, Katcha, he had only seen briefly, but he did leave her with a small present. Their child would be born nine months later.

His absence from Tokyo was to be covered up. While travelling back to Japan, he made sure to stop by in Germany, in order to confirm his status as an ardent Nazi. Visiting Germany would allow him some element of cover when returning to the German community in Japan, as well as giving him the chance to buy a number of small tokens as evidence of his visit. He also briefly stopped in the Netherlands and paid a visit to his remaining family members, a mother, and a sister. The passport he had used to travel to Russia was destroyed and, once again, he journeyed under his real name. Sorge reached Tokyo on the 26th of September, 1935. This was to be the last time he ever visited Europe or America. Back in Tokyo, however, his spy network beckoned him closer.

A Deadly Pact

And so, Richard Sorge returned to his work in Japan. Over the coming years, he worked hard to perfect the network. Clausen was integrated into the team and became a far more dependable outlet for radio communications. This allowed Sorge to increase the amount of information that was being fed back to the Soviets. Ozaki, buoyed by his new position at the newspaper, began to foster better and better contacts, eventually getting close to the Prime Minister of Japan. The network constructed by Sorge had at its heart the German Embassy. Ott's position as an unsuspecting cog in Sorge's machine was cemented when he was so impressed by one of Sorge's reports about Manchuria that he sent the full article (and gave credit to Sorge) all the way back to Berlin. The brass in Berlin were equally as impressed, and from thereon they were keen to read anything Sorge produced. Sorge's Nazi credentials were immaculate to the extent that one might reasonably assume him to be working undercover for the Germans. This duplicity was at the heart of Richard's Sorge's incredible spy work. While the majority of undercover agents might play one role exceptionally well, Sorge's existence was a web of increasingly complicated pretenses. He was an actor, performing a play within a play within a play.

But for his superiors, the ultimate threat of the invasion of the Soviet Union remained the key preoccupation. As such, the demand was always for information about potential collusion between Japan and Germany in moves against the USSR. Despite Sorge's exquisite intelligence examining the outbreak of war in Manchuria and how it pertained to Russia, perhaps more impressive was the manner in which he unearthed information about a secret pact between two of the

Soviet's most worrisome nations. In 1937, Sorge's spy network began to produce incredibly important work for his adopted home.

A Position of Trust

1936 brought with it changes in the German embassy, such as the arrival of a man named Dr. Hans-Otto Meissner. He was to be the Third Secretary at the Embassy, and as was now customary, it was not long before he was introduced to Richard Sorge. The journalist introduced himself with a tipped glass and a comment about the "oriental paradise" into which Meissner had arrived. The manner in which Sorge had talked to him – never mentioning a name – seemed to indicate that it was taken for granted that he would be well known enough.

The arrival of Meissner was an indication of the scaled-up diplomatic relationships between Germany and Japan. The young diplomat was part of a wider expansion requested by Hitler at the time, with the Asian country becoming particularly more important to German plans. The Nazi's Foreign Service had sent a number of its most promising young diplomats out east and Meissner, son of a diplomat himself, was one of them. Despite the widening of the Germany social circle in Tokyo, Sorge remained at its heart.

This was how he conducted his espionage. While films and TV will have us believe that spies are typically involved in outlandish heists and covert operations, history's greatest spy functioned almost entirely in a visible fashion. Sorge was a talker and a communicator. He could speak to people on almost every level and quickly gain their trust. His manner of manipulation bore fruit when these people would turn to him and seek his advice on a variety of matters. Revealing their information, Sorge gave his opinion and analysis before sending this intelligence back to high command. It was complicated, balanced on a razor's edge, and devastatingly effective. But not everyone was so seduced.

Of two other arrivals at the time, one grew close to Sorge and the other kept him at a distance. The former was Lieutenant Colonel Friedrich von Schol, who journeyed to Japan as an assistant military attaché. Ott, as ever, introduced him to Sorge, and the two discovered that they had fought together at Ypres. Even if Schol had entertained reservations about the journalist he had met, he was liable to grow close to a man whom he had fought alongside during the World War I. The two began a growing friendship.

Not quite so successful was the meeting with Count Ladislaus von Mirbach-Geldern, who was set to head up the embassy's press department. He arrived with a letter introducing him to Sorge, written by an associate in Berlin. However, the two men's personalities clashed. Mirbach seems to have considered Sorge's lifestyle – a heavy drinker and a keen socialite – to be adverse to his way of thinking. While the two were both servants of the press (or so it seemed), they would work together without really bonding. A more stoic type, descended from an old aristocratic family in Bavaria, Mirbach kept his distance from Sorge and was content to never develop anything more than a professional relationship.

For Meissner, however, Sorge was fascinating. Unlike anyone whom he had ever met, the journalist seemed to be both repellent and attractive all at once. Writing later, he described the undercover spy as a "dissolute adventurer," someone who possessed a "brilliant mind" at the same time as an "unassailable conceit." He noted Sorge's womanizing, as well as the fact that he was a key figure within the social scene, accepted everywhere. Perhaps most telling were his observations regarding Sorge's close working bond with Ott, and that to snub Sorge was to snub Ott by proxy. Meissner operated under the belief that Ott held Sorge to be some type of secret agent (working for the Germans) and thus indulged him. Despite his reservations, he confessed to finding it hard to resist Sorge's "obvious high zest" and approach to living.

This position of trust within both the German social and Embassy communities meant that, in 1936, Sorge was the first to hear when Ott made a major discovery. Coming across the particularly enormous problem, Ott ran straight to the small office in the building that had been set aside for Sorge to use. Bursting through the door, he requested that Sorge walk with him to his own office, where the huge news would be delivered.

A Secret Pact

As soon as Sorge was safely stashed away in Ott's private office, the German attaché began to excitedly tell his friend about everything he'd just learned. After talking with sources at the staff headquarters of the Japanese Army, Ott had heard of secret talks between countries being held all the way across the world in Germany. Talking through Admiral Canaris, both Hiroshi Oshima and Joachim von Ribbentrop had entered into initial discussions that were to be held in the greatest of secrecies. Up until this point, neither Ott nor Dirksen had been at all outwardly aware that their home nation and their host nation might be tentatively feeling out one another, preparing an agreement that could become an alliance. Ott had just found out about the negotiations, and running to his friend, had a special job that only Sorge might be trusted to complete.

It was Ott's plan to send a telegram – coded for secrecy – to the General Staff HQ back in Germany, requesting that he be allowed into the loop and be told exactly what was happening. He needed Sorge to help with the message's preparation, but only on the strict condition that his friend tell absolutely no one. Quite obviously, Sorge was more than happy to help. The pair secluded themselves away in Ott's home, where they enjoyed even greater privacy than at the Embassy. Secrecy was incredibly important to Ott, and so the message would be read by no one other than the two men. It was telling of Sorge's espionage skills that he had so carefully constructed a situation in which German state secrets were rushed into his hands before almost anyone else in the Third Reich knew of their existence. By this time, Ott trusted Sorge more than almost any of his Embassy staff. Sorge's spell over the Germans in Japan was cast and in full effect.

Once the message was coded and written, it was telegrammed directly to Berlin. The pair waited and waited, but no reply was forthcoming. Ott began to suffer, worried that he had made the wrong move. Fearing for his actions, he finally decided to approach the Embassy head, Dirksen, and reveal the information that had arrived at his doorstep. Dirksen was sympathetic to the attaché's plight and encouraged him to check again with the headquarters, this time using an alternative Army code. Dirksen agreed with the importance of the matter and also with the fact that they could reveal the information to very few people. Only Ott and Sorge were to know anything, he ordered.

Again, Sorge was more than happy to assist Ott with the writing of a second message. They wrote out a brand new telegram and coded it in the alternative manner. This time, their efforts were successful. Or at least, partially successful. The German General Staff replied with a message that informed Ott that they were unable to reveal much information in the contents of a telegram. If he wanted to learn more, they suggested that he would do well to visit the Japanese General Staff in person and request additional information.

Of course, throughout the entire process, Sorge had been updating his Russian superiors with the latest news. Their fears regarding a potential military agreement between the two nations seemed to be justified, and at least in the preliminary stages, Sorge had brought them evidence of this pact coming to fruition. Every step of the way, Sorge had been transmitting radio broadcasts back to Russia, informing them of every single development from within the walls of the Embassy. It speaks very highly of Sorge's espionage abilities that the Soviet Union was so fully informed of these negotiations before practically every person in Germany and Japan outside of a select band of trusted officials. Thanks to their agent's work, the USSR was better informed of Japanese and German foreign policy than many of the countries' own diplomats, officers, and politicians.

But Sorge went a step further. He knew the news of a potential alliance between the two nations would be incredibly threatening to the USSR, with a military-political pact being exactly what his superiors had long feared. Russia, Sorge knew, was clearly the target intended by the alliance. As such, he found himself naturally against such an agreement and resolved to do something about it. He worked without the knowledge or permission of the Fourth Department, using his ties to the Embassy offices to work outside of his capacity as a journalist and associate of the staff. Knowing he held the confidence of both Dirksen and Ott, he began to argue that the allegiance proposed between the two nations was, in fact, a bad plan. Making use of his rhetorical skills, his insight, and his intelligence, he attempted to steer the two men towards a critical view of the pact, hoping their negative outlook would be passed up the chain of command.

Setting Out to Destroy

Sorge continued in his discussions with Dirksen and Ott. Up to this point, he had been happy to offer the occasional piece of insight and to take a back seat. But now, Sorge began to become more and more active in his conversations with the two men. In particular, he recalled the history lessons of his youth, bringing to mind the teachings of Otto von Bismarck that had enraptured him at an early age. He reminded the two Embassy men of the German diplomat's foremost policy: that Germany must never, under any circumstances, risk the possibility of engaging in a two-front war involving Russia and France. Should Germany be caught between east and west in such a manner, victory would be almost impossible, as proved during World War I. Instead, Sorge advised, Germany might be better to tie itself in with the Russians in order to better cope with the threat of Britain and France. He also pointed to information about Japan that they all knew but that might not be familiar to those back in Berlin. Namely, recent political troubles in Japan meant that internal problems were intensifying, with many of those inside the military not worthy of trust. If Germany were to enter into a military alliance with the Japanese, it could be considered quite dangerous under these conditions.

But Sorge's own personal knowledge came to the forefront when he began to dispel notions within Germany and Japan that Russia was in a particularly weak moment. The overriding theory among German and Japanese think tanks suggested that an imminent collapse of the

Soviet government was possible, and that the Red Army was merely a shadow of the threat it seemed to pose. These concepts, Sorge told Ott and Dirksen, were simply not true. Moreover, the alliance itself was likely an attempt by men such as Ribbentrop and Oshima to further their own causes and push for professional advancement at the expense of their countries. Sorge pushed the theory that the entire matter was down to private ambition, as opposed to a mutually beneficial national policy.

Perhaps the most important part about Sorge's interjection was that he was correct. From both his nominally German and secretly Russian viewpoint, his insights were accurate and his analysis thorough. But the issue was that the decision to pursue the pact between the countries did not lie with either of the two men he had been trying to convince. Ott, in particular, was swayed by Sorge's analysis of the current condition of the Japanese military and the dangers involved with making such a pact.

For Dirksen, the news of the possible alliance was not exactly shocking. For months, there had been mutterings of the potential for such a deal emerging from the upper echelons of Japan's General Staff. Determined to discover more about the matter and believing himself to be able to actually offer useful insight as the head of the German Embassy in Tokyo, he departed for Germany in April of 1936. He aimed to both clarify the rumors that Ott and Sorge had encountered, to impart his own view to the high command and to seek out a cure for a bout of asthma that had been troubling him in recent months. He left, his head now filled with Sorge's interceded analysis of why the alliance might not be in Germany's best interests.

On arrival in Germany, however, Dirksen discovered that the Foreign Office was not quite as well informed as he had thought. The bulk of the negotiations thus far had involved just three parties: Wilhelm Canaris of the High Command Intelligence Service; Hiroshi Oshima, a Japanese military delegate working in Berlin; and Joachim von Ribbentrop, who bore no official connection with the Foreign Office but was directly linked to Hitler. In effect, the German Foreign Office had been kept out of the loop and were very interested to learn about the plans Dirksen brought to their table. Realizing the scope of their lack of knowledge, Dirksen began to probe deeper into the Foreign Office's opinions of the deal that had just come to light. He found that, like Sorge, they were vehemently opposed to such an alliance. Other government departments such as the War Ministry also held reservations about Hitler's growing relationship with the Japanese.

Tense Negotiations

Despite – or perhaps because of – the secrecy surrounding the deal, progress on any kind of pact was slow. Meeting in Berlin, Ribbentrop, Oshima, and Canaris decided that they might send a delegate out to Japan to visit Tokyo and take stock of the feeling in the country. They wanted to know whether the Japanese government, such as it was, would be keen to fall in line with the military in sealing the pact, as well as finding out just how strong an ally Japan would be in a partnership with Germany.

The man they chose was Dr. Friedrich Hack. Hack was not technically a government employee. Rather, he worked for the Heinkel Aircraft Company. He did have previous experience in such a role, however, having spent time working for Ribbentrop as an agent when scouting out the original deal with Oshima. Hack arrived in Tokyo and began to get a feel for the city and the happenings within Japan. To begin with, he seemed reserved about approaching Ott with his questions. After Ott revealed that he was fully aware of the deal, the delegate was seemingly more willing to discuss the nature of the issue with the Embassy's military attaché.

Hack and Ott spent a great deal of time going over the deal and Ott learned much about what was proposed. Chief among the problems he mentioned was the German Foreign Ministry's reluctance to draw themselves too closely to Japan, or at least as closely as Ribbentrop's proposed deal seemed to indicate. The negotiations back in Berlin were dependent on Hack's intelligence-gathering mission, and this added to the additional time that was being spent over the deal. Nothing would be signed until Hack could give a full report in person, assuaging the fears held by the various German government departments.

An added comic element arrived when Hack began to chat to Sorge about the affair. The German doctor revealed to the confident that a number of Soviet spies had been noticed standing outside the residences of Oshima, Ribbentrop, and Canaris. When speaking to Sorge, Hack confessed that the Soviet suspicions had grown to the extent that Hack himself had been used as a go-between when the trio were trying to establish the early details of what would eventually become the Comintern Pact. His efforts had helped the Japanese and Germans evade all of the Soviet's attention, Hack confessed to the Russian spy.

As was to be expected, Sorge passed on this information to his superiors, and he then believed that Hack himself began to pick up an increasing number of trails. While it was likely untrue, Sorge would later claim credit for turning the Russians on to the negotiating trio. Soviet agents in Germany would make a habit of following the three (plus Hack), and while fueled by Sorge's information, they were likely already aware of at least the major players in the pact, if not the exact information of the nature of their alliance.

Continuing through the spring and summer of that year, Ott shared numerous reports with Sorge. One of the most interesting was a document detailing the extent to which Japan might be able to commit to a war with Russia. Soon, Ott colluded with Sorge to put together his final analysis on the matter. He supposed that, of the eight or nine divisions that Japan had positioned in Manchuria, the total amount was not sufficient to fight a war against Russia. Should the Japanese Army move their remaining forces (which totaled sixteen divisions), they were still not likely to be able to withstand a large-scale conflict. If they were to cope with such a war, they would need a great deal more training as well as improved border fortifications, better weapons, and other improvements. He concluded that it was slightly too early for Japan to wage such a war, and as such, it was slightly too early for Germany to consider entering into a military alliance with the Japanese.

Thanks to the combined efforts of Dirksen (who had brought the German Foreign Office in on the matter) and Ott (who had sent a damning report with Sorge's assistance), many of the more extreme elements of the proposed treaty had been significantly scaled back. The Soviet Union, thanks directly to the influence and intelligence of Richard Sorge, could sleep better in the knowledge that the military alliance between Germany and Japan was looking increasingly unlikely. This was the case, right up until Hitler took to the stage as the Nuremberg Party Congress of the Workers' Front that September and proceeded to launch into an infuriated rage against the evils of Bolshevism. The gathered German diplomats listened as their leader railed against everything the Soviets represented.

Previously, Hitler had contented himself with constant barrages against one of his favorite enemies: the Treaty of Versailles. Already occupying the Rhineland in flagrant dismissal of the Treaty, however, he turned towards another of his favorite targets and let it be known to all in attendance that he considered communism to be one of the chief threats to the German nation. Thus, the Foreign Office was suddenly tasked with the need to turn the Fuhrer's impassioned language into a slightly more diplomatic and reasonable tone without weakening their leader's position.

This was a particular problem for the man recently appointed to the post of Ambassador to Moscow, Count Friedrich Werner von der Schulenburg. He gathered around his fellow diplomats and began to ruminate on the icy reception he was likely to receive when he returned to the Russian capital, the air still filled with threats issued by the leader of the Third Reich. Dirksen was still in attendance at the Congress and spoke to Schulenburg. Dirksen, ever the biting cynic, congratulated Schulenburg on the fact that he might be able to take it easy from now on, as no one would reasonably expect him to be able to reason with the Soviets whose very existence now seemed to be deeply offensive to Hitler. Luckily for the newly appointed Ambassador, this turned out to be exactly the case, and he was content to simply travel around the more European reaches of the USSR and mingle with his Soviet equivalents. Dirksen, seeing the extent to which Russia was now on the agenda of the German leadership, returned to Tokyo. His asthma, which he had briefly managed to tame

while in Europe, instantly returned to him as he resumed his posit
Japan.

A Considered Victory

For Richard Sorge, the matter was to be classified as a resounding victory. His intervention had turned the tide of official opinion and had guarded against one of his superiors' greatest fears, a military alliance between Japan and Germany. When the eventual agreement emerged from the discussions that he had observed from afar, it took the form of the Anti-Comintern Pact. Announced via official channels on the 25th of November, 1936, the agreement between Japan and Germany seemed to be fairly superficial. It was a political alliance, designed to foster the sharing of information regarding the activities of the Comintern, as well as a collaborative effort to put together preventative measures for Soviet interference. A number of other states were invited to join in the treaty and accept similar anti-communist measures. It was to remain in effect for five years, up until 1941, with both countries agreeing to take extra steps when attempting to curtail the dealings of individuals who were serving (both directly and indirectly) the Communist International.

There was a stringent denial from both parties that there were any secret clauses hidden away in the pact. Despite these denials, there was indeed additional agreements. The secret clause agreed that, should one of the two nations face an unprovoked attack (or even the threat of an attack) from the Soviet Union, then the other would be required to refrain from measures that might "be apt to relieve the position" of the USSR. Rather, both nations would begin consultations as to how they would maneuver to preserve their common interests. Furthermore, it was forbidden for either state to enter into any kind of treaty with the Soviets that might compromise the Anti-Comintern Pact, unless it was mutually agreed by both Germany and Japan.

But the Soviets refused to accept that the surface-level clauses of the Pact were the final product. After twelve months of tough negotiations, there had to have been something agreed that would be of more significance. Indeed, we know that the Ambassador to Japan, Konstantin Yurenev, told his American equivalent that the Soviets possessed firm evidence that there was a hidden military pact in addition to the political terms. This was backed up by the information that Sorge had passed along, as well as the common sense assumptions of the importance of such secret meetings. Yurenev confessed that this belief really did set back the progress of Russia's relationship with the Japanese.

For Hitler, however, the pact was a step closer to his ambition to thwart communism throughout the world. As one of a number of fascist states, he began to entertain the idea of collective security when dealing with the threat of the Soviet Union. The Anti-Comintern plot was one element of this. For Japan, the benefit lay in releasing some of the pressure that their isolationist stance prompted by their departure from the League of Nations and the animosity towards their rule following their invasion of Manchuria. For Japan, this was confirmation that they would not be alone should the Soviets threaten war.

As the German Ambassador to Japan, Dirksen was expected to make a report regarding the Japanese reaction to the Pact. As was almost standard practice by this point, Sorge was able to photograph the report before it was sent, and it arrived on the desks in Moscow and Berlin almost simultaneously. In this report, Dirksen detailed the internal splits in Japan that prevented them from agreeing to anything more decisive. While there had been the intention to forge a true military alliance between the two countries, these internal conflicts had diluted the deal into its current state. The weak commitments laid out in the secret clauses were unavailable to the public, while the lack of anything concrete in the public version of the document meant that many members of the public criticized the deal as being weak and pointless. It was of Dirksen's opinion that such hostility would eventually die down among the public and political organizations.

The Impact of the Pact

But the aftereffects of the Anti-Comintern Pact would play an important role in how Russia operated on the world stage in the coming years.

They were certain that they must avoid the possibility of a war on two fronts. Almost every diplomatic decision revolved around the importance of this belief. Despite the secret nature of the agreement between Japan and Germany, the Soviets knew that the military pact did indeed exist, even if it was not as strong as it might have been. It was Sorge's gathering of intelligence on the matter that helped heighten the USSR's preoccupation with the existence of the military pact, and as such Sorge had a direct influence on the shaping of Russia's foreign policy. As well as this, his advice to Ott and Dirksen influenced the Pact itself, meaning that he was one of the most influential people in the creation of the Anti-Comintern Pact despite hardly being present.

Of all Sorge's espionage efforts in Japan, this case was an example of his solitary work. Typically, information would arrive from sources such as Miyagi or Ozaki, but Sorge's own contacts brought this intelligence right to his office. Despite the far reaching web of his intelligence net, this operation rarely left the very center. In this respect, he was to be congratulated by his bosses. He was not to be expected to influence foreign policy, but simply to report it. In this instance, entirely through his own work, he managed to document and report data, even prompting changes that benefitted his employers. While many spies would be content to simply obtain a small amount of information every now and then, Sorge remained entirely on top of intelligence that flowed both ways during the Japan-Germany negotiations. Due to his unique skill set and incredible mind, he had established a situation where he was not only able to collect intelligence, but to prod and probe his contacts in order to achieve a desired result. Even though other spies had managed to accomplish great feats of daring do, few had managed to have quite this level of global influence. But perhaps the biggest challenge for Sorge was yet to come. Eventually, his help would be needed to win a war.

Threats from All Directions

Returning to the story in 1940, a great deal had changed. As well as the outbreak of the World War II in 1939, the perpetual standoff between Stalin and Hitler increased awareness on both sides that war was a very real possibility. Added to this, Japan's position amid the tension meant that Sorge was incredibly busy. His intelligence network was thriving with Voukelitch, Clausen, Miyagi, and Ozaki all flourishing within their respective roles and opening themselves up to greater and greater amounts of intelligence. Furthermore, the Embassy had undergone a change in leadership. Dirksen had departed the scene, and in his place Ott had stepped into the number one role. Now, Sorge was not only at the top of a growing espionage ring, but he was also the most trusted confidant of the German Ambassador to Japan. With the Soviet Union worried about attacks from both countries, he was perfectly placed to gather information. With anxious moments ahead, the emergence of something named Operation Barbarossa began to demand a great deal of his time.

Rumors and Whisperings

By the summer of 1940, Ott and Sorge had never been closer. Both had risen the ranks in their professional careers and had become mutually dependent on one another. Through Sorge, Ott had developed a keen understanding of geopolitics while Sorge received unprecedented access to intelligence he would otherwise never have seen. Backed up by the reports of Japanese life and culture he received from Miyagi and Ozaki, he was incredibly well-informed, more than happy to demonstrate his intellectual capacity, and always on hand with analysis for Ott. His prestige as a journalist had also increased. He had published over forty articles in the previous twelve months alone, the majority of which had been front page pieces in Frankfurter Zeitung.

The embassy has enjoyed a staff reshuffle and the latest military attaché to enter the fray was a man named Colonel Alfred Kretschmer. He had been told, as many others had before him, that he would be able to trust Richard Sorge, whom he would no doubt meet in shortly. German diplomats in Japan had one clear goal: to convince Japan and China to cease their current, technically unofficial war. Their arguments were that the war in Europe would soon be over, meaning that the Chinese would no longer be able to rely on the backing of Britain and America. Instead, Japan could depend upon Germany to provide post-war assistance. Talking to both sides, German diplomats attempted to ease the war in the region to a close in order to welcome Japan as a more prominent player in the global conflict.

The reason for this had largely to do with what was considered top priority; top secret work being conducted by Ott and his various attachés. They were working on a plan, conceived by Germany, which involved the Japanese attacking British-owned Singapore. This would have the effect of splitting Britain's navy between two theatres, allowing Germany to gain a temporary hold in the Mediterranean and the Atlantic, thus finally being able to land on British soil with a number of troops. It was the job of the German embassy to convince Japan that a war against the British and an attack on Singapore would be very much in their interests. As ever, all of this was well known to Sorge, and he relayed this information back to the Soviets.

In order to better understand the situation and develop a convincing plan to take to the Japanese, Ott needed to study the issues that a Japanese invasion of Singapore might involve. As Sorge related, the theory suggested that it was possible to take the island if it were attacked from the direction of the Malay Peninsula. If this were to be achieved, then the attack would need to be sudden and would need to allow for at least three months to conquer the island. Germany suggested that she would heighten activities in Europe and thus protect the Japanese forces from the full attention of the British.

Despite the huge amount of planning involved in presenting a comprehensive battle plan to the Japanese, Ott and his staff were met with indifference. Though ultimately unsuccessful, the incident demonstrates the extent to which the Soviets were aware of even potential military battle plans between Japan and Germany. But there was something else to be gained by carefully analyzing the plans. As Sorge looked over the materials, he wondered why Germany might be so insistent on involving Japan in the war and in Singapore in particular. He deduced that the incident was indicative of a clear, repeated desire among the Germans to wage war against Russia. With the information he had at hand, it seemed that Japan attacking Singapore would thus divert British attention and allow the Nazis the effort and the manpower to begin waging war in the east on an unprecedented scale. While Singapore was the objective, Russia was ultimately the target.

Added to this, Sorge was able to acquire knowledge of a series of meetings between German and Japanese officials. While the visit of the German delegation to Japan was public knowledge, the actual content of the meetings was a secret. But there were no secrets from Sorge. He soon learned that the officials were negotiating for Japan to acquire new tanks, submarines, and other weaponry from their fascist counterparts. These negotiations were on-going for many months and seemed to indicate that Japan was preparing for a large-scale military operation. Sorge made sure to update his superiors about every new development.

It has been claimed that Sorge's first communication to Russia that Germany intended to attack came as early as November in 1940. This has been difficult to verify, however, and is likely not true. Rather, the confirmation of what would eventually become Operation Barbarossa would arrive soon after.

Hitler's Plans

It had already been decided in the mind of Adolf Hitler that Germany would invade the Soviet Union. The idea had preoccupied him during the early years of the war, and in December of 1940, he issued what is known as Directive 21, which outlined a plan to attack Russia. It was codenamed Operation Barbarossa. Though the plan had been drawn up, Hitler was quickly realizing that he would have to delay. Noticing this, Hitler came to Stalin with an offer. Along with Italy and Japan, he and Stalin would carve up much of Asia. This was the first of a two-part scheme. The second part involved the invasion of a number of Eastern European countries. These invasions were able to fulfil the Nazi's pre-war objective of Lebensraum (living space for the German population), but moreover, they allowed the Germans to move large numbers of troops into the area without arousing the suspicion of the Russians. The USSR was tentatively interested in the prospect of such a pact and agreed to hear out the Germans.

The agreement was laid out as such: the Soviet Union agreed to recognize the leadership of Italy, Japan, and Germany throughout East Asia and Europe, who would in turn agree to recognize the USSR's territory. None of those who signed would assist countries considered to be enemies of those in the alliance. Secretly, parts of the world were divided up. Italy was to take North Africa and Germany would take Central Africa. Russia would receive the Persian Gulf and the Indian subcontinent. Japan would receive the South Seas. Russian negotiators working on the deal began to demand more and more (typically at the expense of Japan), leading negotiations to fall apart. It was another step in the breakdown of ties between Germany and Russia, another indication that war might be inevitable. However, it cemented the idea in Stalin's mind that Germany and Hitler held no designs on invading Russia.

Despite the collapse of the agreement, Germany was still pushing hard for Japan to enter into the war. However, Japanese and Russian relations had begun to thaw in the wake of the pact, to the point when – in March of 1941 – a Japanese delegate to Moscow prepared to offer

Russia a pact of nonaggression. The Russians batted back with the suggestion of a neutrality pact instead. The Japanese delegate decided that he would continue his round trip to Berlin and learn about what the Germans were offering before committing to any one deal. At the time, the German high command was debating just how much of Operation Barbarossa they should reveal to the Japanese. Hitler overruled attempts to bring the Japanese into the situation, however, worried that they might sell the information to any of Germany's enemies. Still, however, they pressed for Japan to invade Singapore. The actual launch of Operation Barbarossa suffered an unexpected set back in March, when the Yugoslavian revolution withdrew the country from the Axis powers and altered the landscape of Eastern Europe. Nevertheless, the Japanese – having listened to the Germans' suggestions and some heavy hints about their plans for Russia – returned to Moscow and signed a neutrality pact with the Soviets.

This, for Sorge, was a success. It kept apart the possibility of Germany and Japan attacking on two fronts. Sorge wanted to know how the treaty was being received in Japan, so tasked his network – chiefly, Ozaki – with finding out this information. Over the course of a number of meetings with the top agents in his espionage network, Sorge learned that the politicians were divided in their opinion of the matter, though largely in favor. The military presented no objection, while some far right groups were not pleased. As far as general citizens went, they were largely positive, out of fear of a war with Russia. One of the biggest dissenters was a powerful faction within the army. In all, it seemed opinion was largely positive, though divided in place.

This was the view that Sorge fed back to the Soviets. It was his summation that diplomatic relations might be able to divert war, should they be aware of any plans at least two months in advance. If they knew one month before, then the military movements could be handled to ratify the defenses. Two weeks advance knowledge would allow for some defensive preparation, while just one week would be able to "minimise the sacrifice." When he asked Ott directly, the neutrality pact was unexpected and unwelcome from the German perspective. To further Ott's displeasure, the Japanese had abandoned the idea of attacking Singapore. Sorge and the Russians, it seemed, had won this round. They had quelled issues with Japan, annoyed the Germans, and prevented the circumstances in which the Nazis might attack. As ever, Sorge's insights allowed for the Soviets to remain on top of both German and Japanese thought process and intelligence. Over the entire process, however, the still hazy specter of Operation Barbarossa loomed.

Sharp Dangers

While Richard Sorge had seen success on a global level in 1940, there were problems emerging closer to home. His past as a member of various communist parties in Germany was being closely examined by certain factions within the Nazi Party. This was beginning to present difficulties. But thanks to the usefulness of many of Sorge's reports sent to Berlin from Tokyo, the chief of the DNB – Wilhelm von Ritgen – ventured out to his local security branch and attempted to find some way to make these issues disappear, so that he might continue to make use of Sorge's services. His request had the reverse effect, revealing to the Germans that – while Sorge's past did not confirm that he was an agent for the USSR – they had enough to be concerned about. But still, Sorge was too good a source. The men in Berlin determined that they would continue to use Sorge and his work, but under strict conditions. The Gestapo would be held from the door, but Sorge's work was to be thoroughly checked and the man himself placed under observation.

The only man suitably trained enough to conduct the observations was a Gestapo agent who had just arrived in Tokyo as a police attaché. Colonel Joseph Meisinger was despised by many fellow Nazis, with one going so far as to consider him one of the most evil among all the agents in the Gestapo. Insults such as "practically inhuman" were levied against Meisinger, who had a record that was shocking even to Heinrich Himmler, who had demanded that the man be court martialed and then executed. But somehow Meisinger had escaped death and had been sent to Tokyo. Informed about the potential duplicity of Sorge, he was given his task. He was to observe the apparent journalist and convey regular reports back.

And just like that, Sorge suddenly had a threatening new enemy, officially sanctioned to work in the very Embassy he had come to call home. As with any new recruit, Sorge worked to quickly set up a working relationship with the man and the two became something approaching friends. For Sorge, a close eye on the Embassy's police attaché was a matter of course. For Meisinger, it was a mission in and of itself. Following closely on the heels of a request for information on Russia, China, and Japan, however, it was more than enough to spark Sorge's suspicion.

As such, he began a campaign to charm the newcomer. The two worked their way through a large amount of the Embassy's whiskey stocks, with witnesses observing that Sorge was willing to offer a friendly joke or two about Meisinger's weight. While the Gestapo agent perused through the files left by the previous person in the position, he came across a paper Sorge had signed, a receipt for a small payment. This could be a legitimate expense payed to him by the Embassy, or it might indicate that Sorge was actually an agent for some German branch. It was impossible to know, so Meisinger had to be careful. As he reported back to his own superiors, Sorge was believed to have the confidence and favor of everyone at the Embassy and had built up outstanding connections among the Japanese authorities.

With Operation Barbarossa looming ever larger in the German's plan, Sorge's reports were increasingly important. That was why, when a police officer questioned one of the German officers whether he might be observing his own men, Meisinger was ordered to be even more careful. It was assumed the Japanese policeman had been referring to Sorge, but this was never made clear. It was likely, however, as the Japanese police soon began to develop interests of their own. They researched Sorge, as well as any Japanese citizens he might come into contact with. There was little for the Japanese military police – named the Kempeitai – to ponder, but even the suggestion that the Germans might be looking at their own was enough to demand investigation. Anyone who interested the Gestapo, they reasonably believed, would interest them too. Their suspicions involved the concept that the Nazis had arranged the entire thing as a setup, and that Sorge was in fact a German agent. But they investigated nevertheless.

Security in the Embassy was increasing at the same time. Since the outbreak of the war, the population of the branch has risen by the hundreds. There were now reporters everywhere, all delivering their findings to Ott. It was far from the social club it had appeared when Sorge arrived, with grenade-equipped guards now stationed on twenty-four hour duty. Sorge, though, maintained the trust of almost everyone. By this stage, he was practically part of the furniture. With more and more people filling up the buildings, it became difficult for Sorge to conduct his espionage. It was increasingly hard to find an empty office where he might photograph some secret documents, for example. With the Fourth Department growing increasingly busy with news from elsewhere in the world, however, the increased brevity of Sorge's reports was not criticized.

Ignorance Is Far From Bliss

Operation Barbarossa was now a certainty in all but name. To an educated, analytical mind like Sorge, the pieces were falling into place and pointed towards an imminent attack. In April of 1941, Sorge sent a message to his superiors indicating as much. According to Soviet documents, the message Sorge sent declared that the German military attaché based in Tokyo had mentioned that that a war against the Soviets would begin as soon as the war in the Balkans was over. Similar Soviet documents indicated that Sorge was not the only one suspicious of such an attack, but that he was by far the best agent working towards such a conclusion.

Ozaki was working his Japanese sources for more information, attempting to gain confirmation. He was told that the situation between Russia and Germany was "very tense," though a war in the east would likely not benefit Germany, and so it might not be pursued. But this did not tally with what Sorge had learned elsewhere. Indeed, one of the diplomatic military envoys sent to Japan by Germany was encouraged to answer the question of just how prepared Japan might be to assist in any war. The very same officer, plied by Sorge's charm, confirmed that war was already a "determined fact" and even broke down Germany's objectives as being: 1) occupy the Ukraine and its grain area; 2) capture at least two millions Russians to use for forced labor; and 3) to eliminate the danger posed on the Eastern border of Germany. The complete picture was pieced together from tidbits and scraps from other sources, until Sorge felt comfortable that he knew the entire plan. Mobilization of troops and fortifications being built up in the east all pointed towards an imminent attack.

Throughout May, Sorge's communications to the Soviets grew increasingly certain. One suggested the end of May as the date believed by German officers. There was a huge amount of data to send to Russia, but not all of it was reaching its target. By this time, Clausen the radioman was beginning to have extreme ideological doubts. He admitted to having torn up a large number of the longer manuscripts Sorge had marked for transmission. This was the latest incident after months of sabotage by Clausen. It's been estimated that, since the beginning of 1941, less than half of the material Sorge hoped to send never made it to Russia. The only messages Clausen sent were the ones he was too fearful not to send, the most pressing transmissions.

Sorge was unaware of the development. He continued to find out as much as possible about Operation Barbarossa. From Lieutenant Colonel Schol, by this point an old friend, he discovered detailed battle plans. He knew roughly 175 divisions of Nazi troops were placed on the eastern border, all mechanized or in tanks. He knew that the attack would occur right along the front line, chiefly directed towards Moscow, Leningrad, and eventually the Ukraine. There would be no warning, no ultimatum. Instead, Germany would simply jump straight into war. Germany hoped to break the Red Army in a matter of months, opening up the Siberian Railroad in the winter and freeing up direct contact with Japan. Again, however, Clausen's crisis of ideology meant the message was never sent.

Still in the dark regarding his associate's betrayal, Sorge waited for a response. The information he sent had been scintillating, with the attack seemingly less than a month away. But his warnings were not being heeded. There was no diplomatic effort to avert war, no opening of communications. There was not even a movement of Russian troops. Instead, Sorge received a strange message: "We doubt the veracity of your information." The words sent Sorge into a whirling rage. Clausen, with him at the time of the message, worried that the master spy might ask Moscow just how it could ignore his thoughts, that he might ask for a breakdown of everything he had sent in order to be sure. Such a move would have doomed Clausen, but it never came. Sorge was too angry to think straight. The message was an insult to Sorge's skills, a dagger to his vanity. Added to this, he was genuinely concerned for Russia's future. How could they not listen?

Having devoted his best years to establishing a spy ring in Japan – a task thought impossible – and having provided some of the greatest intelligence of the war, Sorge was now being ignored, and worse, his competence doubted. The incident took a huge toll on Sorge. It strained his nerves, led to him finding annoyances in the tiniest of details, such as the voice of a new maid. He drank more than his usual, already heavy amount. Despondent and feeling alone, Sorge was at his lowest ebb. He would never truly recover. To him, it might have seemed as though the man who had chosen between Russia and Germany (and then dedicated his life to the decision) had cast the wrong lot, all while pretending to work for the other side. As a German, he should have been delighted. As a Russian, he was worried. As a professional spy, he was destroyed.

War

Russo-German tensions reached a fever pitch. In the Embassy, it seemed everyone knew that war was imminent. There were those who worried for the condition of their colleague, Richard Sorge, who had quite obviously begun to exhibit signs of suffering. Ott, in particular, attempted to engineer a move back to Berlin for his old friend. Even after being drowned in the Embassy's whiskey supplies, Sorge refused. Not only did he hate the Nazis, but he had no interest in being simply another journalist. In Tokyo, his position made him a celebrity.

In Germany, he would be entirely insignificant. Added to that, his secret career made such a move impossible.

Sorge still labored in a professional capacity. He attempted to send further details to Moscow, but these were obfuscated by Clausen. Eventually, Sorge resigned himself to the fact that the war was coming. As the events Schol had predicted began to unfold, he decided that he must best dedicate himself to preventing Japan from also attacking the Soviets. Added to this, Sorge's output as a journalist never ceased. It may have been a coping mechanism for the huge amounts of stress and pressure at the time, but he managed to write fifty-one articles during the first six months of 1941.

On June the 22nd, 1941, Operation Barbarossa was finally launched. Sorge consoled himself by drinking heavily. Having managed to pull himself together somewhat to return to work, there was one night when he was up late discussing the matter with Clausen. Why, Sorge demanded, had Stalin not reacted to his repeated warnings. Indeed, the Russian leader had seemingly missed many alerts to the impending invasion. American and British spy networks had caught similar stories and passed them on. Russia's own spies had offered up information. And, most damning of all, Sorge's reports were deemed to be unreliable. There are reports that Stalin trusted Hitler right up until the moment of the invasion, and after he was proved wrong, locked himself away from the world, so shocked was he by the German attack. For Sorge, the outbreak of war was worsened by the idea that his own reports might have reached Stalin's hand, only to be ignored. There have been suggestions that Stalin was quoted as referring to Sorge as the "bastard" who spent years setting up "brothels and factories" in Tokyo, refusing to believe the reports. Incidents such as these paint Stalin as a paranoid, delusional leader, unable to grasp the importance of his very best agent.

After Operation Barbarossa launched, Sorge continued in his work. Now at war, any indication of German or Japanese plans was just as – if not more – valuable. But Sorge was not the same man. The event broke him, in many respects. With pressure and suspicion of his own activities coming from Germany and Japan, as well as inside his own

Embassy, it is a miracle he managed to continue to work. But it is a tribute to his innate abilities as a spy that he was able to function so well despite his apparent mental breakdown.

For example, he was able to inform the Red Army that there were three conditions that must be met before Japan attacked Russia: 1) the capture of Moscow; 2) the Kwantung army reaching three times the size of its Russia equivalent; and 3) a civil war breaking out in Siberia. Information such as this allowed the Army commanders to assuredly remove forces from the eastern border to add to those battling the Germans in the west. Messages such as these were important in the Battle of Moscow, for example, which inflicted the Nazi's first major loss in their Russian escapade. Of all the spies working during war time, the information Sorge provided at this point may have been the most important anywhere in the world. In many ways, it allowed the Soviets to gain a foothold in the fight against the Germans. As this tide was turned, so was the outcome of the entire war.

Similar successes helped the Soviets win the Battle of Stalingrad, one of the most important battles in all of human history. It is reasonable to say at this point, that the work undertaken by Richard Sorge in Tokyo in the 1930s and 1940s was the greatest accomplishment by any spy, ever. The achievements and depth of information were breathtaking. It was only through betrayal – by Clausen, by his superiors, and by Stalin – that his work did not have a greater impact. Already a heavily damaged man, however, Sorge would not live to see the end of the war.

The Fall of History's Greatest Spy

As a spy, much of Richard Sorge's work was conducted far from the investigative eyes of those around him. By 1941, he had spent so long as the German journalist that he had, in essence, become him. There was little pretense about the cover story any more. Open criticisms of the Nazis were astonishing to those who met him for the first time, but familiar to those who knew him. These phrases – which would be enough to provide most Germans with a visit from the Gestapo – were explained away as minor quirks of character. The charm and social cunning of Sorge the spy allowed him to essentially hide in plain sight.

But this loudly quiet approach to life meant that there was little ceremony surrounding his arrest. The entire premise rested on the idea that he was more useful alive to everyone than he was in any other condition. Even the Germans relied upon his information, the Japanese on his analysis. But it would be the latter that finally caught up with the Soviet spy.

Arrest

For the entirety of his time in Japan, Sorge had used unbreakable radio ciphers. The messages Clausen was sending (when he deemed fit to work) were impossible for foreign powers to read. Nevertheless, the broadcast of the messages themselves was sometimes heard and – even if they were not understood – they aroused suspicion among the Japanese. It was suspected that a spy ring of some sort had been established, though they had no indication of its size, scope, or owner.

One of the first men captured was Ozaki, then a close trusted friend of high ranking politicians. He was taken into custody on the 14th of October, 1941. Immediately, the Japanese military police began to interrogate the Japanese agent, extracting as much information from him as they could.

Richard Sorge was arrested just two days later. Unbefitting of a man who had spent years as the planet's foremost secret agent, the investigation and arrest were surprisingly benign. Perhaps if Sorge had not been quite so resolutely broken by the events surrounding the German's attack on Russia, there may have been more pomp and circumstance surrounding the capture. Less than 24 hours later, Ott was notified that his trusted friend had been arrested by the Japanese under suspicion of spying. Clausen had been arrested alongside his superior officer. In spite of his growing disillusionment with communism, he had not revealed Sorge's secret.

Ott was shocked and outraged at the same time. He figured it to be a case of the typical Japanese hysteria that surrounded many espionage cases. Rather than spying for the Soviets, Ott assumed that Sorge had been caught passing information to German agencies regarding dealings between the Americans and the Japanese. Growing anti-German sentiments within Japan's government might also be blamed. He pledged his support to the local authorities and promised to investigate with immediate effect. The full scope of Sorge's Soviet betrayal would not be revealed for months. During this time, he was interrogated, questioned, and very likely tortured.

Sugamo Prison was to be Sorge's new home. Just like Ott, the Japanese investigators initially assumed that their prisoner was nothing more than another Nazi spy. His membership to the Nazi Party and his German ancestry seemed to point them in that direction, indicating that he was likely an Abwehr (a German intelligence organization) agent. All attempts to contact the German division, however, were met with denials. After spending time under torture, Sorge finally let the veil of mystery fall a final time. He confessed to being a Soviet agent. Finally, Sorge was no longer forced to live behind the banner of the lie that had dictated his life for the last two decades.

But the Japanese were not finished with him. Rather than death, Sorge might be a useful commodity. Three times, the Japanese attempted to contact the Soviet Union. They intended to propose a trade: Sorge for one of their own agents. Each time, however, they were met with the answer that the Soviets had no idea who the captive man was. They rebuffed Japan's suggestions each and every time.

Death

And so it followed that Richard Sorge had no use to any country. Any home he had ever known now disavowed his existence. Russia refused to maintain the possibility that they might know who he was. Germany resented the betrayal of one of their star intellectuals. Japan hated the fact that this man had so successfully built up an intelligence network right under their very noses. Caught in the hinterland between the three countries, Sorge was transformed from one of the most important men in the world to a useless product, a spent case ready to be thrown in the garbage. It was almost three years before the Japanese finally decided that there was nothing more than could be extracted from the captured spy, that he had nothing left to offer the world beyond his death.

He was hanged on the 7th of November, 1944. The time was 10:20am. Earlier that same day in Sugamo Prison, Hotsumi Ozaki had met the same fate. It would be twenty years before the Soviet Union officially acknowledged that Richard Sorge had been their agent.

Some have argued that Sorge's greatest success was the reason he could not conceivably be allowed to live. In 1941, faced with the admission that he might have been given a clue as to the impending Nazi invasion, there was simply no way in which Stalin might have admitted to Sorge's existence. To do so would be to admit fault, to admit that he had been given prior awareness of Operation

Barbarossa. And so Sorge was left to languish away in jail until such time that he was killed.

Richard Sorge was buried in the prison graveyard. It would be some time before his bones were dug up and taken to a more respectable location in Tokyo's Tama Cemetery. At the time of his death, his mother was still alive and living in Germany. And so ended the story of history's greatest spy.

Conclusion

Commemorative stamp of Richard Sorge
Soviet Union (1965)

Richard Sorge's achievements are incredible. He reinvented what it meant to cultivate intelligence in the modern world. While other spies have conducted more daring operations, or have shot more people, these grandstanding operations pale in comparison to the importance of Sorge's spy network. He was charming, a master of seducing people into a sharing state. He convinced people to bring information to him, eliminating the need to actively seek it out himself. As well as his skills of pure espionage, he was armed with an inquisitive, analytical mind that allowed him to boil down data to its purest form and apply it to the world at hand. A voracious devourer of culture, history, and the world around him, it should perhaps not be such a surprise that such a man became a master of information.

Thanks to the efforts of Richard Sorge, we can legitimately say the world was changed. His espionage efforts and political influence helped shape the foreign policy of three major countries at a time when the countries of the world were at each other's throats. Had he not been met with such resistance from his superiors, or indeed, from within his own network, he might have accomplished even more. For more information on the individual feats accomplished by Sorge and other spies, there is a further reading list included at the end of this book. For anyone else, spreading the relatively unknown story of Richard Sorge can help pay tribute to the hidden story of one of the world's most interesting people and history's greatest spy.

Bundesarchiv, Bild 183-H1106-0025-001
Foto: Brüggmann, Eva | 6. November 1969

The inauguration of Richard Sorge Street in Berlin, 1969

Further Reading

Barth, J. (2004). *International Spy Museum handbook of practical spying.* Washington, D.C.: National Geographic.

Corera, G. (2012). *The art of betrayal.* London: Phoenix.

Deakin, F. (2010). *The case of Richard Sorge.* Faber and Faber.

Humphries, J. (2012). *Spying for Hitler.* Cardiff: University of Wales Press.

Prange, G., Goldstein, D. and Dillon, K. (1985). *Target Tokyo.* New York: McGraw-Hill.

Schoenhals, M. (2013). *Spying for the people.* Cambridge: Cambridge University Press.

Whymant, R. (1999). *Richard Sorge.* Hamburg: Europ. Verl.-Anst.

Whymant, R. (2006). *Stalin's spy.* London: I.B. Tauris.

Photography Credits

Also by Conrad Bauer

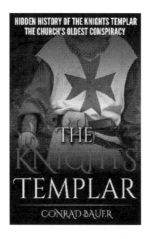

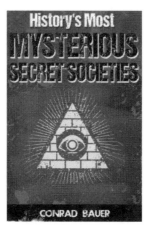

Printed in Great Britain
by Amazon